A-Z of Capacity Management

Practical Guide for Implementing

Enterprise IT Monitoring & Capacity Planning

Dominic Ogbonna

Published by BookLocker.com, Inc., St. Petersburg, Florida.

Printed on acid-free paper.

Booklocker.com, Inc.
2017

First Edition

To my wife Blessing, and my sons, Jeremiah and Godsportion; you are wonderful.

TABLE OF CONTENTS

FOREWORD

Capacity Management is a bedrock of application stability. Collecting the appropriate metrics, understanding the data and reacting in a timely manner can avoid outages or at least reduce the time taken to fix an issue. This book will teach your organization how to ensure metrics are designed from the beginning of the Software Development Lifecycle and deployed to production to collect the necessary insight into the environment.

One of the common misnomers for capacity management is all metrics are driven from the infrastructure. Dominic provides critical insight into how understanding the business needs and capturing the expected profiles drives teams to make better decisions. For example, a set of servers running at100% CPU utilization might look like a problem - unless those same servers are the batch processing systems or grid computing nodes designed for computational analysis. In this case, capacity decisions would be driven by business expansion or volume/timing and the available headroom left on the servers to run more computations.

Dominic has written a thoughtful and detailed book on planning capacity metrics to provide insightful views to your business cases. He provides both the theory of the capacity management processes and the practical implementation that is so often overlooked - using real-world examples and the specific commands. Having seen Dominic's suggestions in practice, the techniques are invaluable to the organization implementing them.

Megan Restuccia
Former Executive Director at Morgan Stanley

ACRONYMS

ATH	All Time High
AVG	Average
BVI	Business Volume Indicator
CDB	Capacity Database
CI	Configuration Item
CM	Capacity Management
CMDB	Configuration Management Database
CPU	Central Processing Unit (the brain of the computer)
CSF	Critical Success Factor
CSV	Comma-separated values
DC	Data Centre
DR	Disaster Recovery
DSV	Delimiter-separated values
DTFC	Days to Full Capacity
EC2	Elastic Compute Cloud (from Amazon)
ETL	Extraction, Transformation and Loading
GB	Giga Bytes
IaaS	Infrastructure as a Service
IMSI	International Mobile Subscriber Identity
IOPS	Input- Output Per Second
IOSTAT	Input/output statistics
IT	Information Technology
ITIL	Information Technology Infrastructure Library
MAX	Maximum

MB	Mega Bytes
MF	Mainframe
MIN	Minimum
MIPS	Millions Instructions Per Second
ML	Machine Learning
MOT TEST	Ministry of Transport Test - an annual test of vehicle safety and road worthiness in Great Britain
MQ	Messaging Queue
MSU	Million Service Units
NAS	Network Attached Storage
OS	Operating System
PaaS	Platform as a Service
PerfMon	Microsoft Windows Performance Monitoring
RACI	Responsible-Accountable-Consulted-Informed
RAG	Red-Amber-Green
RAM	Random Access Memory
RPS	Request Per Second
SaaS	Software as a Service
SAN	Storage Area Network
SLA	Service Level Agreement
SLM	Service Level Management
SME	Subject Matter Expert
SMS	Short Message Service
SNMP	Simple Network Management Protocol
SQL	Structured Query Language
SSO	Single Sign-On
TB	Tetra Bytes
TPS	Transaction Per Second
TCO	Total Cost of Ownership
UID	Unique Identifier
UOM	Unit of Measure
URL	Uniform Resource Locator
XML	Extensible Mark-up Language

PREFACE

WHY I WROTE THIS BOOK

Most often we are told the "**what and why**" of capacity management, but not **how** to make it happen. This book provides good practical approach on **how** to implement the capacity management process, with a view to bringing its benefits to the organization.

The subject of capacity management is now treated like a theoretical process, and as an oral tradition which has lost its right content. It is now common knowledge that a good number of trainers in this process do not understand the basic concept, how much more offering a practical insight.

This book provides a detailed guideline for practical implementation of the capacity management process, with a view to demystify the management process; a move from theory to practice - using a simple capacity management model that can fit into organizations of any size.

Repeatedly, I have seen individuals and organizations very keen on implementing capacity management correctly, but inadvertently, they end up doing it wrong because, traditionally, the focus is just on monitoring and alerting based on the host server resources usage - CPU utilization, Memory utilization, etc. This book seeks to clarify the process and expose the readers to a simplified way to doing it right, while adding value to the organization through capacity management process.

The full benefit of implementing the capacity management process is usually harnessed when it operates as a value-added process within the organization. This will be possible when the process maturity level is well above average.

Capacity management can hardly be accomplished solely by the capacity analysts/manager working alone; to get its implementation right, this book outlines both the technical and business stakeholders that should be involved. It also contains questions you should ask regarding most IT service/application to ensure you are monitoring the right business and service data.

WHO SHOULD READ THIS BOOK

This book is for anyone who wants to have an in-depth knowledge of how to implement capacity management process in an organization, and those whose functions or services involve mitigating business risk associated with IT service failure.

From a technology point of view, CIOs, CTOs, capacity managers, capacity analyst, capacity planners, business and technical service owners, IT operations managers, service managers , IT and business consultants, IT auditors and risk officers, operation engineers, business managers, senior business managers, application architects and developers, infrastructure support analysts, etc. will find this book very insightful, and useful.

Furthermore, CEO, and senior business leaders who are interested in delivering excellent service to customers, but with focus on reducing IT Infrastructure spending will also find this book very rewarding.

BOOK ORGANIZATION

This book is organised into chapters based on the capacity management process model diagram, with each chapter describes how to practically implement the process. In addition, each chapter has conclusion, success hints and organizational appraisal questions; that are designed to help the reader evaluate the process implementation within their organization.

Chapter 1, What is Capacity Management, introduces capacity management, its goals and benefits, and the need to use business data to drive capacity planning rather than basing it on infrastructure resource usage.

Chapter 2, Capacity Management Strategy, dwells on the guidelines for putting the proper policy and procedure in place to drive the capacity management process.

Chapter 3, Capacity Management Gap Analysis & KPIS, provides an overview of what to look out for when assessing the current state of the process, and how to measure the success of the capacity management process.

Chapter 4, Monitoring and Resource Data Collection, provides ways to go about collecting system resource performance data.

Chapter 5, Business Metrics Data Collection Techniques, provides deep dives for business metric instrumentation, and how to determine the business metrics capacity limits.

Chapter 6, Data Aggregation Methods & Granularity, provides guidelines for transforming the collected metric data to meet the capacity management needs.

Chapter 7, Capacity Database (CDB) & Data Storage Techniques, provides the information that will help towards building scalable and high performance CDB/CMIS.

Chapter 8, Capacity Reports, looks at the report audience and what they need to know.

Chapter 9, Capacity Planning, gives in depth guidelines on how to get started with capacity planning, and the basic inputs and tools required.

Chapter 10, Building Analytical Capacity Planning Model, an extensive guideline for building capacity planning models, and a step by step description of a sample model.

Chapter 11, Capacity Planning Review with Stakeholders, covers how to get the business users' co-operation in the capacity planning.

Chapter 12, The Capacity Plan, guide to writing formal capacity plan document.

Chapter 13, Capacity Threshold Alerting & Response Types, introduces effective threshold breach management.

Chapter 14, Cloud Computing Capacity Management, reviews the place of capacity management in the cloud computing and machine learning era.

Chapter 15, Auditing the Capacity Management Process, how to ensure the capacity management process is kept on track and fit for purpose.

Appendix A, UNIX Server Performance Data Collection Techniques, focuses on vmstat, sar, and iostat; and turning their output to csv format.

Appendix B, Windows Server Performance Data Collection Techniques, overview of Logman.exe for performance metrics collection

CONVENTIONS USED IN THIS BOOK

The following typographical conventions are used in this book:

Italic

   Indicates quotes from people, formulae, command-line options

Italic Bold

   Indicates text that should be replace by the user with the appropriate values

ACKNOWLEDGEMENTS

Megan Restuccia and James Gallacher deserve special thanks for their encouragement and support. Additionally, I am very grateful to Megan for her suggestions that has enriched this book.

I would like to thank Temitayo Arikenbi who dedicatedly used his vast experience in the IT industry to critically review the book, and made meaningful suggestions regarding the book content and its organization, ensuring all categories of reader have a definite take away from the book. I will also like to thank Robert Ravenhill.

Special recognition goes to my wife, Blessing, a very special person, whose love, support, encouragement, dedication, companionship and proof reading made this book possible. My sons, Jeremiah and Godsportion with their recurring question, "Daddy, have you finished the book?", propelled me not to give up on writing this book.

1 CAPACITY MANAGEMENT - ISSUES, GOALS, AND BENEFITS

"Facts do not cease to exist because they are ignored"
– Aldous Huxley.

INTRODUCTION

Capacity management is the information technology risk management process for ensuring there is adequate infrastructure and computing resources to meet the current and future demand of the business in a cost effective and timely manner. This management process primarily seeks to proactively ensure that applications and infrastructures have the ability to provide the resources required to meet the organization's current and future business demand needs in a cost-effective and timely manner. Capacity management is also a risk management technique for ensuring that an IT service meets SLA target in a cost effective and timely manner.

It is one of the processes defined in the Information Technology Infrastructure Library® (ITIL®) framework, and belongs to the Service Design phase of service lifecycle. Within an organization, the maturity level for implementing capacity management can vary for different IT services used by the business depending on their criticality to the business.

A desired maturity level is where the capacity management process can be proactively applied to support the business' current and future demand without reacting or fire-fighting to restore IT service outage or performance degradation arising from inadequate IT resources to cope with the business demand. This implies that to attain this maturity level, capacity planning will not only be driven by the current utilization of the IT infrastructure resources, but also by how the future demand of the business will affect the infrastructure resources utilization. Resultantly, at this level of capacity management maturity level, capacity is represented using terms that the business users understand, and not technical jargons.

Capacity management is not only about having adequate infrastructure resources for business, it is also about right-sizing and cost-savings; by ensuring that excess capacity provisions are detected and retracted.

Having a good capacity management process in place is not an antidote for preventing IT service incidents, because IT service outage or performance degradation could arise from other sources - human, coding, or IT change management errors, etc. As a result, the capacity management process key-performance-indicators (KPIs) should be based on eliminating incidents with capacity risk as the root cause.

BENEFITS OF CAPACITY MANAGEMENT

Capacity management brings about the goal of right-sizing the application and infrastructure resources, by aligning the current and future business demand at the right cost. There are several other benefits associated with it when correctly implemented, amongst these are:

- IT organization provides services to the business with increased efficiency and at reduced cost because IT expenditure is planned, and excess infrastructure capacity eliminated
- Reduce the Total Cost of Ownership (TCO) of IT Infrastructure
- IT service failure arising from capacity risk, performance degradation, or SLA violation is eliminated
- Provides senior management the assurance needed for operational, tactical, and strategic growth planning
- Increased productivity
- Organization enjoys goodwill from satisfied customers arising from service reliability and dependability
- For some applicable business sectors, helps with compliance to external regulatory requirements; and the elimination of penalty linked to compliance failure.
- Reduced licensing costs from planned upgrade, and excess capacity reduction
- The business users get involved with the planning of their infrastructures supporting them, no longer unilateral decision by the technical departments.
- Ensure a moving away from reacting and fire-fighting to planned IT infrastructure upgrade
- Provides resource utilization versus business demand information that helps with application tuning activities; and revealing instances of poor coding, database query, or system architecture
- Supports rapid business growth
- The reduction or elimination of service outage or performance degradation incidents with capacity-as-cause, helps to boost the morale of the application support team; and makes them more focused
- Provides centralized point for capacity management process auditing, for all applications/systems within an organization

- Makes it easy to transfer infrastructure and computing resources from places of excess capacity to where needed, without additional spend
- Capacity management helps in the development of the application performance testing function within an organization
- Increases customer or end-user experience satisfaction, loyalty, and retention
- Provides data needed for incident investigation, and problem root cause analysis.

HOW DOES CAPACITY MANAGEMENT NEED ARISE?

The need for capacity management has arisen because IT infrastructure and computing resources are limited in supply; increasing these resources will usually involve the organization parting with money. In contrast to the limited resources, the demand for them increases as the business grows. As a result, capacity management deals with **balancing** IT infrastructure, computing, and processing resources along:

- Cost of getting resources versus resource capacity available
- Supply by IT providers versus demand by business users.

These are further illustrated below.

Practical illustration:

You have an application that can allow up to 1000 online buyers logins at the same time, and operates with performance service level agreement of login average completion time of within 3 seconds. The cost of upgrading the application to maintain the stated service level agreement is $5000 for each additional 100 buyer-logins.

Cost versus Capacity scenario
- If the current capacity is 1000 (maximum logins)
- Any attempt to increase the concurrent logins beyond the current capacity of 1000 will require spending more money - a cost to the business
- Increasing IT processing capacity always has cost implication for the organization. The cost could be both fixed and recurring.

Supply versus Demand scenario
- If the current capacity is 1000
- If the monthly peak concurrent buyer-logins over the last 6 months is 200, it will make sense to reduce the capacity, and increase it as demand increases. (this will not only save the business money, it may also reduce other licensing costs associated with this application)
- If on the other hand, the business as a result of new marketing plan informs you that in 6 months time, it expects the buyer-logins to increase by additional 500. At this point, you will need to increase the capacity to accommodate the expected demand increase, however, you need to carry out a planned upgrade close to the expected demand increase
- Increase or decrease in business demand of an IT service should translate to IT infrastructure resources supply upgrade or downgrade respectively.

COMMON ERRORS IN IMPLEMENTING THE CAPACITY MANGEMENMT PROCESS

There are some common mistakes often made while implementing the capacity management process they should be avoided if you desire to get the full benefits of the process.

- No single capacity planning model will be a fit-for-all applications or systems
- For infrastructure resource utilization or service latency, the maximum aggregated value is good for monitoring the system heart beat and incident investigation. However, it is not good for capacity planning. The resource utilization spikes could come from system panic, bad database queries, system command, application bug, or other unexpected sources. As a result, using the maximum aggregation method, a single or transient spike in resource utilization will erroneously be taken as the value of the periodic data set, rather than getting the peak utilization incurred over a sustained time interval. This will lead to infrastructure over provisioning or excess capacity which is a cost to the organization
- Like above, the average value is also wrong because it obscures the real high utilizations over the period interval. This will lead to infrastructure under provisioning or inadequate capacity which is a cost to the organization
- Modelling infrastructure resource utilization, for example, 'Total CPU utilization' using trend line will lead to inaccurate planning, because such resources' response time will no longer operate linearly once the CPU is overloaded
- Capacity planning based on only Infrastructure resources utilization may never be representative of the business volumes and throughput driving your infrastructure capacity, and will lead to inaccurate planning
- Business capacity metrics without performance measurements, (throughput and latency), will not be able to provide the needed end-user perception of the IT service
- Capacity Planning should be carried out based on peak trading period metrics
- In data collection the focus should be on measuring resource used, and not resource available. Capacity management is about reporting, and planning based on resource utilization
- Collecting resource data for which there is no known capacity limit or specified available maximum capacity will not be useful in capacity

management, as the focus is to know how much of the available capacity is in use

- As much as possible, capacity management reporting and alerting data should be based on percentage utilization of the target resource rather than absolute measurement value

- Capacity planning should not overlook any aspect of the application's computing or infrastructure resource because the overall capacity is determined by the least capacity element or component. Just as any part of a car not properly cared for can cause a car to fail MOT test, same applies to capacity planning; any IT application component without enough processing capacity can result in capacity-caused incident affecting the entire application

- To successfully implement good practice based capacity management, you must be ready to evangelize, and covert the traditional ("this is how we do it") capacity planners in the organization – who will quickly tell you that they monitor their servers CPU and disk spaces utilization, by informing them of the added advantages the new implementation, will bring to the process.

- It is desirable for an application to drive CPU utilization to peaks near 100%, over short duration; this confirms among other things that the hosted application:
    - Is maximizing the use of the CPU resource, and is not CPU bound
    - Is multi threaded
    - Is optimized to take advantage of multiple processor cores
    - Can be scaled vertically by adding more processor cores, or replacing the processor with a higher frequency one.

CAPACITY MANAGEMENT VERSUS CAPACITY PLANNING

Usually the terms 'capacity management' and 'capacity planning' are used interchangeably, this is not right. In summary, capacity planning is a subset or component of capacity management. Capacity plan is the output from the capacity planning component; and implementing the capacity plan is the end product of proactive capacity management.

Capacity planning is usually done in consultation with the business users/representatives that provide their business demand forecasts as an input to the process; which in turn predicts the infrastructure requirement to meet the future business demand.

Capacity management adds value to organizations when it can proactively help mitigate service performance degradation or outage relating to inadequate infrastructure resources.

At the lower maturity level of capacity management, there may not be explicit capacity planning process in place, rather the IT support team relies on infrastructure utilization threshold alerting, and users' IT-service-failure complaints. This approach is reactive, and leads to fire fighting for service restoration.

COMPONENTS OF CAPACITY MANAGEMENT

Capacity management process like any other information technology management process has building blocks, or components. The key components of the capacity management process are shown below in Figure 1.1 (Dominic's model of the capacity management process diagram); each of the components will be described in detail in subsequent chapters. The components are shown as hierarchical model so as to show the relationship and interconnection between them. All of the components working together will usually deliver the main benefits of implementing the capacity management process.

All or some of the listed components of the capacity management process can apply to an organization depending on the size of her information technology estate. Similarly, depending on the organization's size, some of the components and the responsibility for them may be combined into one.

As shown in the Figure 1.1, some components are grouped together in a container that is theoretically and commercially called different names, among them are: capacity database (CDB), or capacity management information system (CMIS); in this book, CDB is adopted. A typical CDB application may be able to provide some or all the functionalities of the iterative activities of the enclosed components. It should be known that most of the commercial CDB applications are more focused on Infrastructure resource data analysis and reporting; with little or no focus on capacity planning that is based on business data. A mini-CDB implementation can provide the functionalities expected from some of the components shown in Figure 1.1.

Figure 1.1 Capacity Management Process Diagram - Dominic's Model

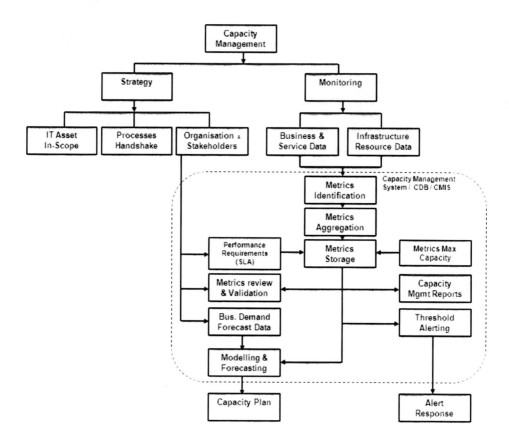

Each of these components or group of components is discussed in detail in the subsequent chapters.

SUMMARY

The capacity management process is an IT service risk management technique, which should be given adequate attention, so as to ensure that service failure or performance degradation arising from inadequate infrastructure resources is proactively and cost effectively eliminated. This can happen when:

- In this digital age, customers can easily switch service, capacity management should be seen as a business enabler, not only as cost centre
- Organizations should embrace the capacity management process, and give it the needed senior management support.
- Capacity management should not be seen as just reacting and fixing capacity issues arising from infrastructure resource threshold breach alerting. It should be proactive, by focusing on the business capacity drivers which are causing the resources usage to increase.
- The capacity management process is incomplete without the capacity planning component, which makes the process proactive.
- The capacity management process is also aimed at reducing the cost of doing business, by eliminating excess infrastructure provisioning, licenses, and other associated costs.

ORGANIZATIONAL APPRAISAL

1. Is capacity management process implemented in your organization?
2. Is the capacity management implementation yielding the expected benefits?
3. Is capacity planning part of your capacity management process activities?
4. Is your capacity management process determined by business volumetric or just system resource utilizations?

2 CAPACITY MANAGEMENT STRATEGY

"For every problem, there is a solution that is simple, neat, and wrong"
- Henry Louis Mencken

"Strategy is a commodity, execution is an art "
- Peter Drucker.

INTRODUCTION

Senior managers' support is required to implement an effective capacity management process that will bring value to the organization. For this reason, it is important to have in place an agreed strategy.

Strategy ensures that the process gets the needed support, involvement, and contribution from the various stakeholders. It also provides a mandate for the capacity management team to drive the process towards excellence.

The following should be covered in the capacity management strategy document (the organization's capacity management policy):

- Capacity Management Maturity, and plan to attain the target value level
- Specify IT asset scope to be covered and the criteria for the determination
- Identify the capacity management stakeholders and organization

- The expected handshake between capacity management process, and other IT management processes.
- IT services' basic requirements for capacity management compliance

These are discussed in details.

CAPACITY MANAGEMENT MATURITY MODEL

The capacity management maturity model is shown in Figure 2.1. The model shows the various implementation levels of the capacity management process, which an organization can set as a target and value associated with each level of implementation.

As the maturity level increases, the value derived from the process also increases and makes capacity management move from reactive to proactive. Proactive here implies that incidents that would have been triggered by inadequate computing or infrastructure resources are eliminated through planned capacity increase.

The timelines in the model is an indication that often it takes more time to move to the service and value levels; with the value-level taking the most time to attain.

Figure 2.1 Capacity Management Maturity Model

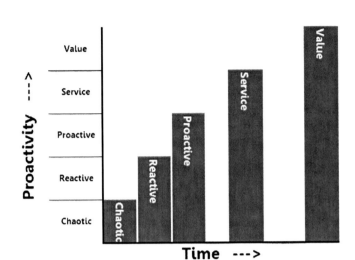

The benefits accruing from each of the maturity levels are shown in Table 2.2. The higher the organization moves in the proactivity scale, the more benefits it derives from the capacity management process.

Table 2.2 Capacity Management Maturity Models Benefits

Benefits / Maturity Levels	Chaotic	Reactive	Proactive	Service	Value
Ad hoc, or no capacity planning in place	✓				
End-users notify IT dept of service incidents	✓				
Host server resource monitoring		✓			✓
Resource utilization threshold alerting		✓			✓
Reactive capacity upgrade		✓			
Application level monitoring			✓	✓	✓
Workloads characterisation			✓	✓	✓

Table 2.2   (continued)

Benefits / Maturity Levels	Chaotic	Reactive	Proactive	Service	Value
Resource utilization trending to predict when capacity should be added			✓		
Monitoring capability across application components			✓	✓	✓
Capacity reporting based on computing and infrastructure resource utilization			✓		
Managing capacity based on IT service view				✓	
Service Level Agreement is defined				✓	✓
Relate computing and infrastructure resource with IT service usage				✓	✓
Predict infrastructure need based on service usage				✓	
Report capacity based on service usage				✓	
Report capacity based on business demand					✓
Relate IT service usage with business demand					✓
Predict Infrastructure need based on IT service usage, and business demand forecast					✓
Meet regulatory reporting requirements for capacity management process					✓
Establish formal capacity management periodic business review					✓
Establish process for capacity management data quality process management					✓

HOW TO DETERMINE ASSETS IN-SCOPE FOR CAPACITY MANAGEMENT

In reality, for an organization that has very large IT estate or plant, it may not be practical to include all the IT assets to be covered by capacity management process from the start. The main sources for identifying IT services and IT assets are:

- The service catalogue maintained within the service level management (SLM) process
- IT assets or configuration items (CIs) with their dependencies managed in the configuration management database (CMDB), and maintained by the configuration management process.

Typically there are two main groups for capacity management process asset scoping, namely:

- Application systems to be included in scope (including vendor provided IT services or application)
- IT infrastructure types to be included in scope

Success Hint:

An organization should not be responsible for the capacity management of a third party IT service hosted on vendor managed infrastructure. Rather, the organization should demand that the SLA explicitly and unambiguously meets the organization's performance, and capacity management objective.

Hence, every organization should have ways of determining and ranking its IT assets, so as to ensure that the most critical business assets are in scope at start of implementing the capacity management process. This ranking process will bring some of the following benefits:

- A big win that makes the capacity management process more visible within the organization
- Brings about senior management commitment to the process
- Provides further buy in from the wider organization
- Brings encouragement, and job satisfaction to the capacity management team
- Increased satisfaction for the customers, and users

Among the criteria to determine the ranking of IT assets for inclusion for capacity management are:
- The average number of active users of the IT asset; and number of other IT assets that are dependent on it
- The business criticality of the IT asset
- The business cost (tangible and intangible cost) of the IT asset becoming unavailable
- The total cost of the IT asset
- The number of capacity induced IT incidents linked to an IT asset
- Penalty liability associated with IT asset breaching SLA with customers or users
- IT assets owned by third party service providers should be low in ranking as it is expected the service provider will take care of capacity management (check that it's included in your service agreement)

The scope of capacity management should also include the categories of IT infrastructure that should be covered. Ideally, all infrastructures on which an IT application depends upon should be covered. It is important that any infrastructure considered as constituting a single point of failure should be in scope for capacity management. In determining this scope, it should be borne in mind that an IT application or service capacity is determined by the IT asset with the least capacity.

Among the IT infrastructures that should be considered in scope for capacity management coverage are:

- Host servers and mainframe
- Network
- Message Queue
- Web servers
- Telephony
- Database
- Load balancers
- Middleware
- Storage Systems
- Grid
- Data Centre, etc.

HANDSHAKE WITH OTHER IT PROCESSES

For effective IT service management, the capacity management process must work together with other IT management processes. The capacity management process depends on other processes for input, just as its output feeds other processes. Figure 2.3, shows the relationship, and Table 2.4, provides detailed handshake between capacity management process and other IT processes.

Figure 2.3 Capacity Management & Other Processes Handshake

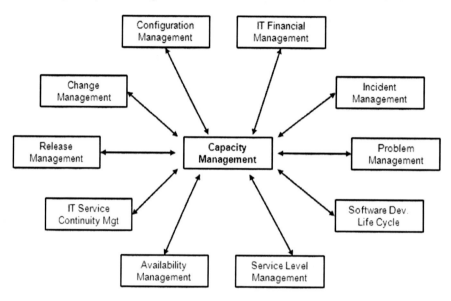

Table 2.4   Capacity Management & Other Processes

Other IT Processes	Relationship with the Capacity Management Process
Configuration Management	• Provides the IT assets inventory and their associated business criticality rating, to guide the assets to be covered by the capacity management process
	• Provides the detailed information needed by the capacity management process; towards identifying all

Table 2.4 (continued)

Other IT Processes	Relationship with the Capacity Management Process
	infrastructure components of an asset.
	• Provides dependency information regarding other assets used or owned by another asset
	• Provides stakeholders information of the asset that the capacity management team will need to work with.
Change Management	• Impact of change management activities deployed on an IT system can further be uncovered by the process, through the capacity management focused post change implementation review.
	• Some changes may result in unintended impacts that may not show up immediately after the change implementation. Thus, few days after the implementation, it is a good practice to review capacity and performance metrics in comparison with baseline.
	• Infrastructure capacity upgrade will also need to go through the change management process. Handles the change risk assessment, and approval processes.
Release Management	• The capacity management process activities may be affected by releases, and can also be used to show the

Table 2.4 (continued)

Other IT Processes	Relationship with the Capacity Management Process
	performance gain or degradation arising from the releases. Releases can also lead to metrics baseline usage changes.
	• Capacity management data provides information to facilitate with the release deployment strategy.
IT Service Continuity Management Availability Management	• Capacity Management should cover assets dedicated for service continuity.
	• Availability management has a lot in common with the capacity management process. Ensuring that high availability options are provided for in application, and single points of failures are eliminated.
	• The goal of capacity management is to ensure that service unavailability caused by lack of infrastructure or computing resources is drastically reduced or eliminated. Degraded service performance is considered as service outage or unavailability.
	• Capacity management reporting and planning should also consider the various availability techniques like mirroring, clustering, and fail over deployed.
	• Liaises with capacity management to ensure there are adequate resources to meet the availability SLA.

Table 2.4 (continued)

Other IT Processes	Relationship with the Capacity Management Process
Service Level Management (SLM)	• Works with the business and application managers/owners to prepare the service performance requirements, and the associated service level agreement (SLA) – target threshold for capacity management. • Manages the service catalogue which helps in identifying IT services to be included in scope for capacity management • The SLA is used by the capacity management process to determine the most appropriate capacity-driver metrics, and the usage threshold; at which capacity risks elimination process could be proactively planned and implemented. • Recipient of capacity management exception reports; and manages on-going evaluation of SLAs.

Table 2.4 (continued)

Other IT Processes	Relationship with the Capacity Management Process
Software Dev. Life Cycle (SDLC)	• Capacity management ought be integrated into every stage of the SDLC, and not an afterthought process. • Architects and developers should think of capacity management from the application design – considering performance and scalability; and hooking up the appropriate metrics instrumentation. • Embedding at application design stage the measurement instrumentations necessary to collect the performance and volumetric capacity driver metrics. • This will also assist during the application's performance testing and further validate the metrics generation hook. • The capacity management process also feeds into the SDLC by highlighting potential bug related system resource drainage. • Regression testing should be carried out after major changes to ensure that performance target is maintained
Incident & Problem Management	• Provides service incident notifications • The capacity management process is very vital for identifying the root cause of most service incidents,

Table 2.4 (continued)

Other IT Processes	Relationship with the Capacity Management Process
	including but not limited to capacity caused incidents.
	• A key performance indicator (KPI) for the capacity management process is the number of incidents with capacity risk as the cause.
	• Capacity-caused incident report help to identify IT assets/applications/systems that should be in scope or prioritized for capacity management process.
	• Designated critical capacity metrics usage breaching SLA threshold should be booked as an incident.
Financial Management for IT	• Helps capacity management with costing options, approvals, and budgeting.
	• For organizations where user departments are charged for IT service usage, financial management provides the calculations, and the administration based on resource utilization.

> *Success Hint:*
> *Performance and scalability requirements should not be left until the time of go-live, or as a tick-in-box for go-live preparedness. These non-functional requirements should be considered at every stage of the SDLC, as a decision at any stage of the SDLC; can upset the performance, and scalability expectation.*

CAPACITY MANAGEMENT ORGANIZATION & STAKEHOLDERS

Implementing effective capacity management process requires a lot of collaboration, and handshake with other IT process owners, and subject matter experts (SME) within the organization. Support and cooperation from other IT process owners is required to make capacity management implementation a success. Table 2.5, shows the relationship.

Table 2.5 Capacity Management Roles & Responsibilities RACI

Roles/Responsibilities	Developers & Architects	Support Engineer	Capacity Analyst	Capacity Manager	IT Auditors	Service Managers	Application Manager	Business Users	Senior Management
Integrated into SDLC Process	R	I	I	I	I	A	C		
Capacity Driver Metrics Identification	C	R	I	A	I	I	C		
Identification of Data sources	A	R	I	CI			C		
Tool Data Feed Format Specification		I	R	A			I		
Metrics Collection script, SQL, or Command-line creation	A	R	I	I			C		
Integrating Collected Metrics to CM Tool			R	A					
Aggregation Methods Determination	C	C	I	R			A		
Data Granularity Determination	C	C	I	R			A		
Service Performance Requirements & SLA Determination			I	I		A	R		
Validate Metrics in Tool			I	R			A		
Data Analysis and Reporting			R	A			C		
Capacity Report Stakeholders			R	A					

Table 2.5 Capacity Management Roles & Responsibilities RACI

Roles/Responsibilities	Developers & Architects	Support Engineer	Capacity Analyst	Capacity Manager	IT Auditors	Service Managers	Application Manager	Business Users	Senior Management
Breached SLA Actions		R	C	C		C	A		
Business Demand Forecast Data – provider			I	I			A	R	
Build Capacity Planning Model			R	A			C		
Develop Capacity Plan			R	A			C	C	
Implement Capacity Plan (scale up or down)	C	R	C	C	I	I	A	I	
Periodic Capacity Reviews				R	I	I	A	C	I

Responsible: the individual who does the work to successfully achieve the task.
Accountable: someone who is accountable for correctly completing the task. The holder of the 'Responsible' role reports to the 'Accountable' role holder.
Consulted: A subject matter expert who provides information needed for successful delivery of the task.
Informed: The people who are kept informed as they are affected by the outcome of the task.
* Depending on organizational size or IT application infrastructure estate, some responsibilities may be merged

BASIC REQUIREMENTS FOR CAPACITY MANAGEMENT COMPLIANCE

Capacity management policy should specify the basic capacity management activities that need to be implemented, before an IT system is considered as having fulfilled the minimum requirement for capacity management. The requirements can include:

- Monitoring coverage for the business sub process, and threshold breach alerting

- Monitoring coverage for the service sub process, and threshold breach alerting
- Monitoring coverage for the resource sub process, and threshold breach alerting
- Storage of the collected metrics in the capacity database (CDB)
- Performance testing is undertaken
- There is defined ownership for the IT system's capacity management
- Business involvement in capacity management, by providing the business demand forecast
- Existence of monthly capacity report, covering business, service, and resource sub processes
- Existence of capacity plan

CAPACITY MANAGEMENT TEAM ORGANIZATION

At the technical level, the capacity management process team will ideally comprise the following:

- Capacity management lead: has the overall leadership for the capacity management process strategy, and the process continuous service improvement
- Capacity Managers: End to end capacity management for designated IT services
- Capacity Planners: capacity modelling and planning, and producing capacity plan for designated IT services
- Capacity Analysts: managing, on-boarding, and support metrics collection from designated IT systems into the CDB; capacity analysis and capacity reporting for designated IT services

The role count for the positions of capacity managers, planners, and analysts will depend on the size of the IT estate. For organization with small IT estate, the above roles can be fulfilled by one person.

To successfully deliver the capacity management process, the roles listed above should establish good cooperation with the IT application and Infrastructure teams.

SUMMARY

The capacity management process will become a valued-added IT service management process, when it is driven by an organizationally approved policy, and supported by senior management. In addition, organizations should set target regarding the capacity management maturity level they aspire to attain.

Capacity management should not be a tick-in-the-box at go-live; rather, it should be integrated within every phase of the software development life cycle (SDLC).

To effectively drive the process, there should be a central point of accountability, and every stakeholder has to supportively play their roles.

ORGANIZATIONAL APPRAISAL

1. Does your organization have a documented and approved capacity management policy?
2. At what capacity management maturity level are you currently operating; and where do you want to be in the next 3 years?
3. What percentage of your critical IT systems is currently covered by the capacity management process?

4. Is there a dedicated capacity management process team in place?

5. Is capacity management process for IT systems initiated at the early stage of the SDLC?

6. Is the capacity management process operating in handshake with other ITIL processes and teams?

3 CAPACITY MANAGEMENT GAP ANALYSIS & KPIs

"Everything's fine today, that is our illusion "
- Voltaire.

CAPACITY MANAGEMENT GAP ANALYSIS

When implementing capacity management policy in a very large organization with vast IT estate, it is generally good to start with gap analysis of the current state of capacity management for the various IT systems and assets. The gap analysis provides the following benefits:

- The current capacity management status of IT assets under review are assessed using common standards and framework
- Along with the IT assets criticality weight, it provides the bases for prioritizing the implementation of the process, and provides direction for the capacity management maturity level to pursue
- Provides foundational information required to plan the implementation of capacity management process for the IT asset
- Bestows the opportunity to meet stakeholders, seek the buy-in for implementing the centralized IT capacity management process with the organization, and also evaluates the stakeholders' willingness to move to a centralized capacity management system
- Presents the opportunity to evangelize the benefits that capacity management will bring to the IT stakeholders, and to the business. Internal IT providers, or IT system managers/owners' interest are kindled towards

centralized capacity management when they know the benefits they stand to gain from the implementation – how it will make their job easier.

Table 3.1, provides a guide of the information that a typical capacity management gap analysis should seek to collect when assessing the current status.

Table 3.1   Capacity   Management   Gap   Analysis   Information

Groups	Details
Application level Capacity Mgmt Contact	• Is anyone responsible for capacity planning for the application?
Business process	• Does the business provide the demand forecast data for capacity planning?
	• Is the measurement data of right business volume driving infrastructure capacity, collected and stored?
Service Process	• Is service performance (latency and throughput) monitored, data collected and stored? For example, response time, Requests/sec, Users/Sec
Resource metrics captured from components	• CPU, Memory, Disk I/O, Disk Utilization, Network utilization, Performance data e.g. Response Time
Monitored Components	• Application Servers, Web/Connection Servers,

Table 3.1 (continued)

Groups	Details
	Database Servers, Firewall, Load Balancing server, Storage, Network
Performance Test	• Is Performance testing carried out? • Is Performance testing integrated with capacity planning?
Forecasting Model Type(s) in use	• None (Production Peak Monitoring), Rule-of-thumb, Trending, Analytical, Simulation
Data Repository	• Do you keep historical utilisation data? • Do you maintain any database for keeping capacity data e.g. Excel, SQL Server, Oracle • Is Data Extraction Automated? • Is Raw Data Storage Automated? • Is Data Aggregation and Storage Automated?
Aggregation methods used & collection Interval	• Keep raw data, Max, Average, Minimum, Percentile, Others Business Volume Indicators, Transaction throughput, Resource Utilisation data, Performance data
Reporting	• Do you have SLA with the business regarding service performance? • Is service level management exception report produced? • Is resource exception report produced? • Is service capacity report produced?

Table 3.1 (continued)

Groups	Details
	• Is there frequency of service capacity reports?
Capacity Plan	• Is Capacity Plan Produced? • Any policy regarding capacity planning review /refresh interval • Is Capacity Plan acted upon? • Is there any major Incident related to capacity in the last twelve months? • Is there any demand management in place influencing the use of any resource?
IT incidents with capacity as cause	• How many serious IT service failures or service performance degradation, are linked to unavailability of the IT resources or computing power? Critical Systems with high rate on this index should make it to the top of IT assets that should be in scope for capacity management.
Relationship / Interdependencies	• Does Incident & Problem Management get input from the capacity process? • Does the Capacity Process get input from Change & Release, or (Change Advisory Board-CAB)? • Is Capacity/Performance Post Implementation Review (PIR) carried out after Change/Release? • Do you get input from Availability management? • Do you maintain any Operating Level Agreement (OLA) with your inputs providers?

Table 3.1 (continued)

Groups	Details
Business Continuity planning (BCP)	• Is the BCP Systems covered by the capacity management process?
Monitoring Tools in use	• Are there tools for monitoring and collecting data for: business volume, throughput, resource utilisation, service performance, and reporting

The Capacity Management Gap Analysis Grading

The gap analysis information collected, should be graded, and analyzed as shown in Figure 3.2. Each grading option should be assigned a numeric value, which will be used to generate the scorecard shown in Figure 3.3.

Figure 3.2 Sample Capacity Management Gap Analysis Summaries

Groups / Details		Weight	App Group 1		App Group 2			
			Application 1	Application 2	Application 3	Application 4	Application 5	Application 6
Asset Ranking		0	High	Medium	Low	Medium	High	Low
App level Capacity Management Contact	Is anyone responsible for capacity planning for the application	2	Yes	Yes	Yes	No	Yes	No
Business process	Does business provide volume forecast data for business indicators	10	Yes	Partial	Partial	Partial	Partial	Partial
	Are actual business volume indicators measured	10	Yes	Yes	Yes	Yes	Yes	Partial
	Critical Business Metrics Needed for capacity planning	0	User Count by Processes	Executions and Orders	Total Message	New Accounts, Total Customers	Total Downloads	Total Orders
Service Process	Is Technical Transaction throughput monitoring in place (e.g. Requests/sec, Messages/Sec)	10	Yes	Yes	Yes	Yes	Yes	No
Resource Utilisation Metrics captured from components	CPU	10	Yes	Yes	Yes	Yes	Yes	Yes
	Memory	8	Yes	Yes	Yes	Yes	Yes	Yes
	Disk I/O	8	Yes	Yes	Yes	Yes	Yes	No
	Disk Usage	10	Yes	Yes	Yes	Yes	Yes	Yes
	Network usage	10	Yes	Yes	Yes	Yes	N/A	Yes
	Performance Time	5	Yes	Yes	Yes	Yes	No	Yes
Type(s) in use	Trending	4	Yes		Yes		Yes	Yes
	Analytical	8	Partial			Partial	No	
	Simulation	10	No			Yes	No	
Data Repository	Do you keep historical utilisation data	10	Yes		Yes		Yes	Partial
	Do you maintain any database for keeping capacity data e.g Excel, SQL Server, Oracle	10	SQL Database	Others	Others	Others	MySQL	None

Caption title: Capacity Management Process Gap Analysis Summary

The capacity management gap analysis scorecard

The information collected from graded gap analysis should be organized in such a way to create a score card view of all systems under review. Figure 3.3, shows a typical capacity management gap analysis output - scorecard.

Figure 3.3 Sample Capacity Management Gap Analysis Scorecards

Capacity Management Process Gap Analysis Scorecard

Groups / Details		Weight	App	App Group 2			App Group 3			Activity Score (%)
			Application 1	Application 2	Application 3	Application 4	Application 5	Application 6	Application 7	
App level Capacity Management	Is anyone responsible for capacity planning for the application	2	10	10	10	0	10	0		66
Business process	Does business provide volume forecast data for business indicators	10	50	30	30	30	30	30		70
	Are actual business volume indicators measured	10	50	50	50	50	50	30		76
Service Process	Is Technical Transaction throughput monitoring in place (e.g. Requests/sec, Messages/Sec)	10	50	50	50	50	50	0		72
Resource Utilisation	CPU	10	50	50	50	50	50	50		80
	Memory	8	40	40	40	40	40	40		70
	Disk I/O	8	40	40	40	40	40	0		60
	Disk Usage	10	50	50	50	50	50	50		70
	Network usage	10	50	50	50	50	50	50		70
	Performance data e.g. Response Time	5	25	25	25	25	25	25		66
Components with	Web/Connection Servers	10	50	50	50	50	50	50		76
	Application Servers	10	50	50	50	50	50	50		76
	Database Servers	10	50	50	50	50	50	50		86
	Firewall	10	0	0	0	0	50	0		10
	Load Balancing server	10	0	0	0	0	50	0		20
	Storage	10	0	50	50	50	30	50		56
	Network	10	0	50	50	50	50	50		60
Performance/Stress	Is Performance testing carried out	10	50	50	50	50	50	50		86
	Is Performance testing integrated with capacity planning	10	30	0	30	0	50	0		32
	None (P... ...ring)				0					10
... Manage... ...produced			21				33			
	Is Resource Exception report produced	7	35	0	0	0	35	0		20
	Is Service Capacity Report Produced	7	35	0	0	0	0	21		16
Capacity Plan	Is Capacity Plan Produced	10	50	0	0	0	50	30		38
	Is Capacity Plan acted upon	5	15	0	0	0	25	0		26
Relationship / Interdependencies	Does Incident & Problem Management get input from the capacity process	5	15	15	15	15	15	15		42
	Does the Capacity Process get input from Change & Release, or (Change Advisory Board-CAB)	5	15	15	15	15	25	15		46
	Is Capacity/Performance Post Implementation Review (PIR) carried out after Change/Release	5	15	0	0	0	15	15		18
	Do you get input from Availability management	5	0	15	15	15	25	15		44
	Do you maintain any Operating Level Agreement (OLA) with your inputs providers	2	6	0	0	0	6	6		28
Disaster Recovery (DR)	Is the DR Systems covered by the capacity process	8	24	0	0	0	0	0		16
Application Total Score		1620	1200	810	951	795	1450	822		
Application Score (%)		100	74	50	59	49	90	51		

CAPACITY MANAGEMENT - KEY PERFORMANCE INDICATORS (KPIs)

The success of the capacity management process can be evaluated using the following indicators; however, the use may vary depending on the current capacity management maturity level of the organization. Table 3.4, describes the KPIs.

Table 3.4   KPIs for the Capacity Management

KPI Item	Description
Capacity Caused Incident	Number of incidents with capacity as root cause
Cost effectiveness	Number of unplanned capacity upgrade
	Number of IT services with excess capacity (infrastructure over-provisioning)
Capacity monitoring Coverage	Percentage of the IT assets already monitored in comparison to the IT assets in scope for capacity management.
Right Business and Service Metrics Coverage	Percentage of IT assets monitored with business and service metrics included
Metrics Data Quality	Percentage of IT assets having good data - data is up to date (no missing data); and metrics usage (%) not exceeding 100% (measurement value not greater than the specified capacity

Table 3.4 (Continued)

KPI Item	Description
	value).
Performance Testing Coverage	Percentage of IT assets for which performance testing is carried out, to determine application limitations and bottlenecks.
Threshold Alerting Coverage	Percentage of IT assets monitored, that have threshold breach alerting / notification configured.
Metrics Review Coverage	Percentage of the IT assets, for which data collection is reviewed and validated by the core stakeholder for correctness.

SUMMARY

Capacity management implementation will likely be more successful if the enterprise or service level gap analysis is carried out prior to implementation. The gap analysis provides the background information against which to plan the implementation.

The successfulness of the capacity management process can be objectively measured; some of the major indicators are number of incidents with capacity as cause; and the degree of IT services covered by the process.

ORGANIZATIONAL APPRAISAL

1. Is there a standard document specifying the criteria that IT systems on-boarded into the capacity management process and tools must meet?

2. Do you periodically review the IT systems on-boarded into the capacity management process for adherence to the specified standard?

4 MONITORING AND RESOURCE DATA COLLECTION

"If you can't measure it, you can't change it"

- Peter Drucker.

INTRODUCTION

IT Infrastructure Monitoring is a system health check process that involves the collection of system resources utilization, performance and availability data. It also involves the analysis and storage of data, and threshold breach alerting. For effective monitoring every component of the infrastructures and their dependencies should be covered.

Monitoring plays key role in capacity management, as it is the source of providing the measurement or utilization data. The capacity management processes goes further to aggregate, and apply the data, in a way it will be more useful in capacity planning.

Based on ITIL framework, monitoring data can be collected for the following sub processes of capacity management, namely:

Business   Collects data that measure the business activities processed by the target application

Service   The application level performance, SLA, latency, and throughput measures arising from the business activities. Focuses on **external** performance metrics based on how the users perceive the service

Resource   The IT infrastructure resource consumption, driven by the application/service usage. Focuses on **internal** performance metrics of the computing resources.

Figure 4.1 Capacity Management sub processes end-to-end flow

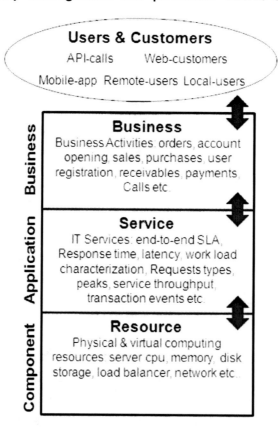

Capacity management report should cover the three sub processes; nonetheless, the report audience will determine the focal point. However, to fulfil the core aim of

capacity management - proactive capacity planning (to predict future infrastructure resources needed to support the business demand forecast), the three sub processes should be used together in a capacity model.

APPLICATION PERFORMANCE ISSUE - THE ROOT CAUSE

The necessity for capacity planning has arisen to combat the performance problems that users experience when using an IT system/application, which sometimes makes such application unusable. It is important to know what gives rise to this performance problem.

Figure 4.2, shows the typical response of infrastructure resource or device to concurrency request types, one example of such device is the CPU. This resource response pattern is what is eventually translated to the external application response, which the end-users experience.

Figure 4.2 CPU Response Time vs. Load/Throughput/Queue Behaviour

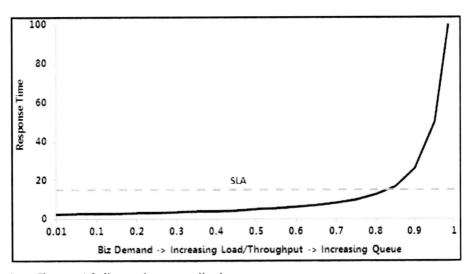

Based on Figure 4.2, it can be seen that:

- The Response time increases as the users' requests increase (e.g. more users requesting a system resource at the same time)
- More user demand leads to additional load, and additional load leads to increased request throughput
- As the throughput increases such that the device cannot respond to all request, the request queue gets increased
- As the queue continue to increase, the device may become unresponsive; and at this point, users will wait almost indefinitely (this state is popularly described by users as 'the system is hanging')
- SLA is breached when the response time stops responding linearly
- One key objective of the capacity management process is to ensure that there are adequate resources to share the load, so that the application will always operate within the SLA acceptance region.

COMMON CAPACITY MANAGEMENT METRICS

There are common metrics associated with each of the three sub processes of capacity management. In this section, we will focus more on the resource and service metrics that are generic. The business sub process metrics are not generic in nature, but vary for each IT application; therefore, detailed guideline will be provided for it in chapter four.

Table 4.3 Common Capacity Management

Sub Processes	Metrics Type	Common Metrics
Resource / Infrastructure	Host/Server	CPU Utilization (Total), CPU Utilization (User), CPU Utilization (System), CPU Utilization (IOWAIT), Queue Length, Memory utilization,

Table 4.3   (continued)

Sub Processes	Metrics Type	Common Metrics
		Number of processes, Disk space utilization etc. In additions, resource performance metrics from Unix utilities - sar, iostat, and vmstat[2;], and Windows longman.exe[3] utility
	Mainframe	MIPS, MSU, CPU Hour, CPU utilization, Paging rates, IOPS, Active Connections
	Data Centre	Total power usage, Cooling, network/internet Pipe bandwidth utilization, space utilization
	Network / Router	Bandwidth utilization, Error rates, packets per second
	SAN	IOPS Usage, Storage allocation Usage
	NAS	Ops/sec, Disk Latency, Storage Pool Capacity, File system capacity
	Disk	Average Seek time, Transfer Rate, Mbytes transferred per second
	Web Servers	Requests queued, Request wait time, transactions per second
	MQ	Queue depth, Enqueue count, Dequeue count, Enqueue Time, Messages/sec, Latency, Duration, Depth high, Enqueue rate, Dequeue rate

Table 4.3 (continued)

Sub Processes	Metrics Type	Common Metrics
	Database/ Database Server	Active Connections, Active Transactions, Queries per second, Average queue length, reads/sec, writes/sec
	Telephony	Number of concurrent internal/external calls, number of calls waiting in the queue
	Load Balancer	Request per second (RPS), Latency
Service[1]	Application	This capacity management sub-process, focuses on monitoring and measuring the application specific function metrics that are quantitatively described: • SLA • Latency/Response Time • Throughputs • Concurrency
Business[1]	Volumetric (Business Volume Indicator)	This capacity management sub-process focuses on business activities that drive the need to add or reduce capacity of the application's dependent infrastructures.

---

[1] This sub process of capacity management will be considered in detail in the subsequent chapter

[2] The UNIX resource performance utilities - sar, iostat, and vmstat are covered in detail in the appendix A

[3] The Windows resource performance utility - longmax.exe is covered in detail in the appendix B

Success Hint:

A host CPU operating at a peak utilization of near 100% is a good thing; as long as such high utilization is over very short duration. Depending on the applications and operating systems, sustained peaks of near 100% (with periodic average of over 80%) can lead to increasing queue, and eventually result in performance degradation.

It is desirable for an application to drive CPU utilization to peaks near 100%; this helps to confirm, among other things, that the hosted application:
- *Is maximizing the use of the CPU resource, and not CPU bound*
- *Is multi threaded*
- *Is optimized to take advantage of multiple processor cores*
- *Can be scaled vertically by adding more processor cores, or replacing the processor with a higher frequency one.*

SYSTEM RESOURCE UTILIZATION OVERVIEW

Capacity and performance data collection is the pivot upon which the capacity management process revolves. Hence, extreme care must be taken to ensure that the data collection, aggregation, and storage activities are rightly done, without impacting the performance of the target infrastructure providing the data. The following tips should be considered:

- The lower the data collection sampling granularity, the better the quality of data collected. Sampling Interval of one second or less should only be used on stable infrastructure, hosting very high frequency applications

- The lower the granularity of the data collection sampling interval, the more it impacts the performance of the infrastructure device providing the data. The common recommended sampling interval are: 15sec 30sec, 60 sec, or 5 minutes

- It is important to clearly understand what the data represents. Is the data provided as:
  - A point time measurement at the sampling interval
  - Average, maximum, or other aggregates of the measurements over the collection sample interval
  - An accumulated measurement, etc.
- A measurement data without a known maximum limit or maximum available capacity value may not be useful, as it provides no basis to determining the utilization level at which to apply performance threshold alerting. Nevertheless, such measurements may be used in providing performance reference point, correlation, modelling, and baseline usage characteristics. Sometimes, system administrators would want to use a server's "Number of Processes" metric to determine the server load; this is completely wrong, because a host server with only 20 running processes can consume more CPU time than when 2000 processes are running
- Focus on collecting measurement data that provides utilization (in percentage), rather than absolute number.
- Data collection across all the dependent infrastructure components must be done at the same time.
- For application with infrastructure components, geographically distributed in countries with different time zones, determining a global peak measurement will require the data collection timestamps getting mapped to the organization's common reporting time zone.

> **Success Hint:**
> Unlike CPU requests that are queued, storage utilization are persistence based requests, hence, its usage at peaks of 100% is risky; it will lead to service failure if the needed storage space is not immediately available.

RESOURCE DATA COLLECTION TECHNOLOGIES

Monitoring systems collect performance data from infrastructure components, devices, or hosts using either agent-less or agent-based technologies. Some monitoring tools support both technologies. Table 4.4, shows the difference between both, and the pros and cons of using any of the technologies.

Table 4.4   Data Collection Technologies: Agent-based vs. Agent-Less

Property	Agent-based	Agent-less
Ease of installation	• Agent must be installed on target host • No remote server is required, more ideal for in-house metrics collection.	• No installation is required on the target host • Remote collection server is required.
Resource usage overhead	• Can add some resource usage overhead to the target host • Collected data is stored locally reducing network bandwidth • Archival of the collected data, if not properly	• No additional resource overhead on target host • Collected data is shipped to the remote data collector, adding to network bandwidth usage overhead • Does not affect the target host storage space.

Table 4.4   **Data Collection Technologies: Agent-based vs. Agent-Less**

Property	Agent-based	Agent-less
	managed, can lead to storage space issue on the target host.	
Security	• More secured, because no external connection to any port is required.	• Connection is required between the target host, and the remote server, additional cost may be incurred to secure the exposed SNMP, API, etc. ports.
Metrics choice Limitation	• Offers broad choice for metrics collections.	• Depends on the available metrics built into the target host, and some applications or targets have no embedded monitoring capabilities.
Central data	• Data is distributed across the various target hosts; thus, the capacity management tool will cycle through each. Conversely, this may not be the case where data from	• The capacity management gets all needed metrics from the remote server.

Table 4.4 **Data Collection Technologies: Agent-based vs. Agent-Less**

Property	Agent-based	Agent-less
	various target hosts are stored away to a central location.	
Data collection failure detection	• More difficult to monitor and alert, when the data collection process fails for each target hosts.	• The remote server can easily track and alert on any target host out of reach.

Success Hint:

The monitoring tools should have minimal resource usage overhead, so that it does not create problems for the system it is supposed to keep alive. The monitoring tools should consume minimal system resources.

RESOURCE DATA COLLECTION METHODS

Application, service, and infrastructure resource usage metrics can be collected by diverse monitoring tools ranging from proprietary, open source, in-house, or a combination of all.

Unlike service and resource sub-processes metrics, it should be noted that business metrics vary for each application system, application architecture, organization, and industry sector. Therefore, there is hardly any proprietary or open source monitoring tool that can automatically collect the business sub-process level metrics. However, the tools could have the capability to extract business metrics from log files built into the applications, or execute some operating system (OS) command or SQL query to extract the data from specified data source embedded into the application at design time. Table 4.5, shows the monitoring tool sources.

Table 4.5   Monitoring Tool Sources

Tool Source	Description
Proprietary	• These are commercial monitoring tools which are usually well supported by the vendors. In addition to the basic monitoring, some commercial tools provide capacity modelling, application level monitoring, capacity database, and reporting. • The commercial tools are expensive, and by default specialize in collecting infrastructure resources utilization data. Hence, organizations purchasing such tool should ensure that the selected tool will be able to support the integration of their business and service metric data.
Open source	• These are free tools that can be downloaded over the internet. Most of them focus on collecting, and monitoring infrastructure resources utilization. • Though they are free there are costs associated with getting the expertise, and the time required to implement them.

Table 4.5   Monitoring Tool Sources

Tool Source	Description

In-house[1]	• These are custom capacity management tools developed within an organization to specifically fit into their capacity management strategy, or IT budget.
	
	• Organizations may decide to develop their tool in-house for the following reasons:
	  o Ease of integrating the in-house tool with other enterprise business applications, security, technologies and integration with other IT processes e.g. service request, incident management, change management, alert mechanism, etc
	  o Ease of modifying the tool to reflect ever changing regulatory requirements
	  o Reduces total cost of ownership (TCO) when compared with implementing a commercial tool for a very large IT estate
	  o Smaller IT organizations may not have the large budget needed to implement commercial tools
	  o Some organizations that are not satisfied with the functionalities provided by the commercial tools may opt to develop theirs.
	
	• For a small IT estate, the in-house monitoring solution can be developed using a combination of scheduled command-line tasks, file storage, simple database, and spreadsheet.

Table 4.5   Monitoring Tool Sources

Tool Source	Description
	• In-house solutions exploit the performance counters built into the operating system, middleware, network, and storage devices. This could be achieved by using the provided in-built monitoring console, command-line, or API.

[1] *See Appendix A for examples of resource data collection using command-line*

RESOURCE LIMITATION TYPES – PHYSICAL AND APPLICATION

Monitoring tools are very good at collecting so many infrastructure resources (both physical and virtual) metrics. However, such metrics will not be ideal for capacity planning if there is no way of determining their maximum limit or total available capacity. Some school of thought will argue that such metrics without any known maximum limit can be used for establishing application baseline behaviour, but using a metric without known capacity limit as baseline can lead to wrong judgement as the performance implication of the increasing trend may not be known.

For example in UNIX- operating system, we have a CPU resource metric called "CPU load" or "CPU load average" ; this measurement increments by 1 each time a new process is using or waiting for CPU resource. This implies that the metrics "CPU load average" is just a number without any known limit; and in reality the "CPU load average" metric may not always have direct correlation with the actual server CPU Utilization. This can be explained by the fact that a server executing a task that initiates 100 processes, can be running at "Total CPU utilization" of 80%; whereas, the same server running a different task involving about 1500 processes will be running at "Total CPU utilization" of 25%.

Resource measurement: absolute vs. utilization value

The absolute measurement value is a number that provides the quantity of the resource measured; for the quantitative number to make more sense, it may be linked to a unit-of-measurement. On the other hand, the utilization measurement is the percentage of the total resource that is used.

Example 1:

If a server has 128GB RAM memory installed, and at a point in time, the server was using 32GB of the installed memory. From this:

- The measurement is for memory
- The unit-of-measurement of the memory is GB
- The absolute installed capacity is 128 GB
- The absolute used memory is 32GB
- The server's memory utilization value, in percentage is:

Memory Utilization (%) = (absolute used memory/absolute installed capacity) x 100

$$= (32/128) \times 100$$
$$= 25\%$$

Example 2:

If a SAN storage system is technically stated to be able to handle 180 Input/output operations per second (IOPS), and at a point in time, the storage system was having 12 IOPS concurrently. From this:

- The measurement is for IOPS
- The unit-of-measurement is none, hence, IOPS is just a number
- The absolute technical IOPS limit or maximum available IOPS is 180
- The absolute used IOPS is 120
- The SAN's system IOPS usage value, in percentage is:

$$IOPS\ Usage\ (\%) = (IOPS\ used/IOPS\ limit)\ x\ 100$$
$$= (120/180)\ x\ 100$$
$$= 67\%$$

From these two examples, it can be seen that stating metric usage as a percentage can be used to harmonize metrics reporting in a uniform and simple term. It is recommended that you go for a monitoring tool that will be able to provide both the absolute and utilization (%) values of a measurement.

Other advantages of reporting resources utilization using utilization percentage are:

- Provides common known scale to report utilization (%)
- Changes in installed capacity of resources will immediately impact and reflect in utilization (%), which otherwise will not reflect, if the report is based on absolute measurement
- It is easy to make decision using utilization (%)
- Using utilization (%) makes it easy to create threshold alerting template with different resources triggering at different usage levels.
- Multiple usage based resource metrics can be plotted on a single chart using same scale

- Utilization (%) based reporting makes it easy for comparative analysis, and decision making

Physical versus Application resource limit

Usually, infrastructure or computing resources could have more than one source of utilization limitations. Namely:

- **Physical or technical limit:** this type of resource limit is imposed by the physical or virtual constraint of the hardware, host container or operating system. Typical examples are:
    1. Server "Total CPU utilization (%)" resource usage metric is measured as a percentage; this implies that the expected maximum utilization is 100%. Ideally, no monitoring tool will collect any usage above 100%.

    2. The RAM memory installed on a computer has a known limit based on the amount of it installed, e.g. 24GB, the memory used can never be above this specified limit of 24GB.

- **Application Limit:** This type of resource limit is imposed by the application; it comes in form of computing components' configuration settings, or by the requirement to meet performance SLA. This is illustrated using the two scenarios below:

Scenario 1: (Capacity limited by configuration)
Apache web server; through its http configuration file setting, you can set the "MaxClients" parameter, which by default is about 256; to indicate the maximum number of concurrent connections to support at any time.

Additional connection requests after the 256 set will be in queue or waiting list – leading to end-user performance degradation.

Scenario 2: (Capacity limited by performance requirement)

In scenario #1, the "MaxClients" parameter could be set at the default value of 256. However, if in the process of performance-testing of the application it is established that the SLA target (having the "Average Response Time" below 5ms) is breached at any time the number of connections exceed 180, the new maximum capacity or capacity limit is now 180 following this.

From scenario #2, which is based on meeting the performance SLA for this application, the total connections available or the connection limit is 180 and not the 256 defined in the current file.

SUMMARY

Infrastructure and computing resource monitoring is a vital component of the capacity management process; however, the monitoring activity is incomplete if the business and service metrics driving the resource utilization are not included.

Resource monitoring solution can be implemented using third party vendors, or implemented in-house. In all implementations, the monitoring should have minimal performance impact on the monitored IT system.

Whenever possible, the resource measurement's absolute and percentage utilization values should be collected. Percentage utilization can only be computed if the measurement's capacity limit is known. Resource measurement with no known capacity limit or maximum measurement value will not be good enough for capacity planning; having said that, it can be used for providing performance reference point and baseline characteristics.

ORGANIZATIONAL APPRAISAL

1. Are your capacity management decisions based on resource metrics with an unknown capacity limit?
2. Are your capacity management decisions based on metrics absolute measurement values, which do not reflect changes in the underlying resource capacity limit?
3. Do you know the performance impact of the monitoring tools implemented for your IT services?
4. Are your monitoring tools configured to collect data at reasonable time granularity?
5. Do you have any process in place, to detect when the data collection feed is broken?

5 BUSINESS METRICS DATA COLLECTION TECHNIQUES

"The secret of getting ahead is getting started"

- Mark Twain.

INTRODUCTION

In the previous chapter, business metrics was briefly introduced and explained, nonetheless, this chapter is dedicated to further discussing this very important and pivotal component of business capacity management.

For an organization's capacity management maturity level to operate in the "value" position, her forecast of IT infrastructure and computing requirements should be driven by the following:

- The ability to measure and express the actual business activities performed by an IT system in business terms

- The business representatives should be able to provide the business demand forecast in business terms

- Capacity reports meant for senior management, and business stakeholders must be expressed in business terms.

The starting point of achieving the value maturity level is the collection of business, and service metrics.

BUSINESS METRICS, CLASSIFICATIONS, AND TYPES

Business metrics are the user induced business activities that drive the capacity requirement of a system or an application. The changes in volume business and user usage pattern are the root basis for infrastructure and computing resource utilization changes.

Business metric classifications

A system could have more than one business capacity-driver metrics; as a result, there is need to classify them accordingly, with a view to ensuring that the best and most appropriate ones are preferentially used in the capacity management reporting and planning functions. The two classes of business metrics are:

- **Principal Metrics** - these are must-have business metrics that are the main capacity drivers of the application. If the principal metrics are rightly identified, any increase or decrease in their throughput will result in corresponding change in the utilization of the infrastructure and computing resources within one or more of the application tiers.

  Inability to collect data on real principal business metrics that directly impact resources utilization will make it difficult to built a reliable capacity planning model.

Given that business metrics are based on business language or terminology, business users understand them, and can provide their demand forecast using the principal metrics.

Consequently, it is recommended that only business metrics in this principal category should be included in the formal capacity management reports meant for senior managements and regulators.

- **Auxiliary Metrics**- other business metrics that are not considered as principal, but that are good-to-have, falls into this class. The auxiliary metrics should be collected if they are easily and readily available, as they may provide information that will further help in capacity management analysis, correlation and modelling.

Business metric types

There are two types of business metrics namely; business volumetric metrics, and service metrics. The Service metrics can further be grouped into two: service performance, and service level agreement (SLA). Table 5.1, provides more details of business metric types.

Table 5.1   Business Metric Types

Type	Category	Description
Service	Performance (Throughput)	• Provides service information of a system; displaying the total activity (functions) done over a unit time e.g. Peak sales count per second, average orders per

Table 5.1   (continued)

Type	Category	Description
		minute, new users per hour, new activations per second, active users per day, connections per 10 minute, concurrency etc.
	Performance (Latency)	• Provides service information regarding the service function performance that are indicative of end-to-end SLA measures e.g. response time, latency, task duration, transaction time, etc.
	SLA	• This capacity management sub-process focuses on monitoring and measuring the application specific metrics that quantitatively describe how well the IT service-function is delivered to the end-users, with a view to ensuring that SLA is met.
		• A clear and unambiguous SLA is usually stated using the combination of both the service throughput and performance metrics, covering both quantitative, and qualitative specifications.
Business	Volumetric (Business	• Business information depicting the total business activity carried out by the

Table 5.1   (continued)

Type	Category	Description
	Volume Indicator)	application over a period e.g. Total daily sales count, Users, Products, Hourly orders count, Monthly users count, New Activations Daily Count, etc.
		• Usually, the business users provide their demand forecast data for capacity planning in volumetric terms.

Success Hint:

The importance of monitoring, and collection of throughput metrics cannot be over emphasized because; IT service incidents induced by capacity problem do occur when the service request throughput is more than the maximum throughput the IT system infrastructure can support.

Business metrics can further be illustrated using this scenario:

Business Metrics Scenario:

1. Company offers registered users online album service, where users can upload as many pictures as possible at any time of the day

65

2. The more users that upload pictures, the more storage space will be consumed on the host node. The used storage space will also be determined by the size of picture files being uploaded.

3. Additionally, as the number of users accessing the online album service, and uploading pictures increases, it will result in the host servers executing more tasks, leading to increased resource usage by the host servers. The resources consumed can include CPU, memory, connections, etc.

4. As the resource usage increases, the time it takes to upload a file will also increase; however, there is a business requirement to ensure that the hourly average upload-time does not exceed 10 seconds.

Scenario Analysis:

1. The principal business metrics are "Active users" and "uploads"
2. The auxiliary business metric is "Total registered users"
3. The service metrics are:
    a. Service performance - throughput: "Active users per Minute" and "Uploads per minute"
    b. Service Performance – response: "Average upload time (sec)"
    c. SLA with business: For total registered users under 10000, the average upload time should not exceed 10 seconds

BUSINESS METRICS IDENTIFICATION TECHNIQUES

As part of the process of collecting business metrics, the application business owners or their representatives (IT system owners/managers/architects) should be consulted to ensure that the appropriate business metrics are collected. After all, the demand forecast data that is required for capacity planning will have to come from the application business owner.

Sometimes, the application business owners or their representatives may not be very clear about how to determine the most appropriate business metrics to be included for data collection. Guidance can be provided using the "question and answer" technique outlined below:

Table 5.2   Business Metrics Identifier Questions & Answers

Probe Question	Typical Answer	Typical Identification Analysis
1. What does the application or system do?	The application receives customer orders, sends out request messages and accepts uploaded files	The likely volumetric business metrics from the stated key end-user activities based on the provided answer are: Request messages, Uploaded files and Customer orders. Note: The identified volumetric business metrics will also have service performance throughput metrics.
2. How do you determine	The time it takes to deliver the request	The likely performance metrics - response time or latency are:

| that activity #1 is satisfactory to the users? | message; and the time it takes to upload accepted files. | Request Message Delivery Time (milliseconds) and File upload time (seconds). |

Table 5.3, shows the outlines of the various business metric types.

Table 5.3   Business Metric Types

Business Metric Types	Identified Business metrics
Business volume indicator [1]	Daily Request messages, Uploaded files, Customer orders
Service performance throughput[2]	Messages/minute, Files uploaded/minute
Service performance latency	File-upload duration, batch file duration, login response time

[1] *can be total over a day.*
[2] *The interval can be 1 sec, 5 minutes, or 1 hour.*

Different applications deal with some peculiar business activities; Table 5.4, lists the likely business metrics that could be driving the capacity of the respective applications.

Table 5.4   Applications - Typical Business Metrics

Typical Application	Likely Business Metrics
Online Sales	Number of sales, number of registered users, number of active users, number of products
Social Media Chat	Number of users, number of active users, number of messages
Stock Trading	Number of orders, number of executions, number of messages
Telecommunication (voice)	Number of active IMSI, call volumes, call durations
Single Sign-on application	Number of accounts, number of sign-on, sign-on duration
Email services	Number of active users, number of emails, email delivery time, number of emails awaiting delivery
Mainframe processing system	Number of records processed, processing duration
ETL application	Number of records processed, processing duration

BUSINESS METRIC DATA SOURCE TYPES

Good business metrics data does not happen by chance; it has to be identified and planned for in the design stage of an application. That is why the capacity management process should be considered in every stage of the software development life cycle (SDLC).

Business metrics data embedded into the application during the design stage provides more suitable capacity and performance metrics that can really help with capacity management. The embedded metrics data collection can be achieved by adding hooks within the application, to get the appropriate data which are written to a file-system or database log.

Detailed time-stamped activity log

Some data collection tools write metric values to the log for each business activity at data point; this provides the data with the lowest granularity. Web servers and custom applications can log metrics at this granularity, with a timestamp field which can be used to compute the service throughout metrics. Care should be exercised in implementing detailed, time-stamped activity logs, to ensure it does lead to tangible performance issue. Detailed time-stamped activity logging can be used to determine both the business and service metrics.

Rather than log every metric data point, the data points can be aggregated over specific time interval e.g. 1 minutes, 5 minutes, 15 minutes, 1 hour or even 1 day before logging them. Depending on the implementation, it may reduce resource usage overhead. Nevertheless, it should be remembered that capacity risk is caused by sustained high usage of resources and, depending on the application's stability threshold, a minute of sustained high usage can trigger service degradation.

Figure 5.5 and Figure 5.6 illustrates a log where every business activity is tracked using the URL POST action; and the query parameters used to pass activity information (3 distinct business activities - purchase, registration, and catalogue are captured in the log).

Figure 5.5 Detailed time-stamped activity log - raw

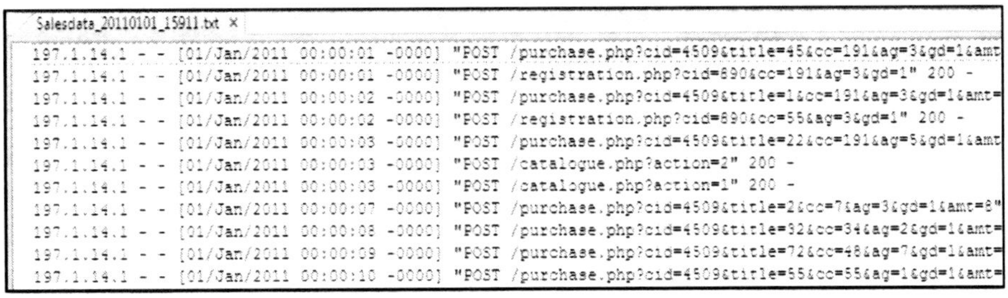

Figure 5.6 Detailed time-stamped activity log - formatted

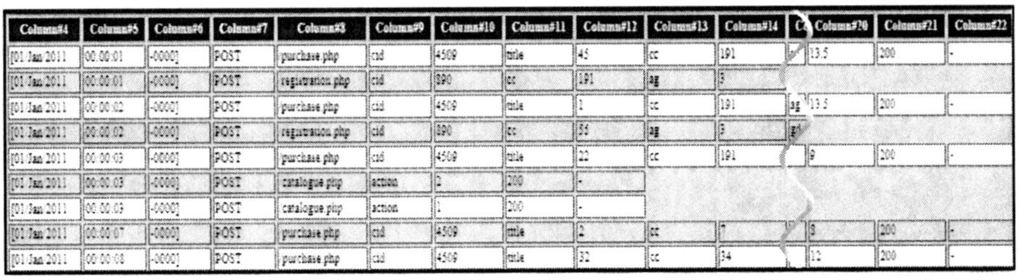

Daily Summary activity log

When an application design does not include capacity management in its development life cycle, getting detailed metrics may be difficult. In such cases, the application may be able to provide only daily summary metrics, as shown in Figure 5.7 and Figure 5.8.

The daily summary metric provides good measure of business volumetric; however, it is not ideal for determining the service's peak throughput number, which is required for capacity planning. Using the daily (24-hour) summary, the estimated peak throughput/second can be calculated thus:

Service performance throughput per second = Total Daily Volume / (24*60*60)

The above formula assumes that the throughput every second is same, which in reality would likely never be true. A more accurate peak throughput/second can be determined by applying a recently computed peak-to-average ratio, thus, using peak-to-average of 1.3 (i.e., 30% more transactions occur at peak sec):

Service performance throughput per second = (Total Daily Volume / (24*60*60)) *

1.3

Figure 5.7 Daily summary activity logs - raw

```
Date,Call Advisor,Team Advisor,Call Offered (Vol),Avg HT (Min),Call Rating (1-5),Blocking Rate (%),Service Level (%),Utilization
(%),adherence (%),AHT Forecast Vs Actual (%),Abandoned Call (Vol),First Call Resolution (Vol),Call PerHour (Vol)
01/01/2014,Laura Mitchell,Linda Carter,8,13,2,5,81,85,100,102,3,1,6
01/01/2014,Todd Wright,Antonia Lamb,14,15,1,2,83,89,97,96,1,0,5
01/01/2014,Deborah Long,Carol Neal,1,5,5,1,86,98,94,102,0,2,10
01/01/2014,Ronald Harris,Caleb Tucker,26,10,5,3,93,90,94,109,4,2,8
01/01/2014,Anna Ward,Lena Roberts,19,6,5,0,93,93,90,106,0,1,5
01/01/2014,Carolyn Flores,Isaac Brooks,19,18,1,1,79,88,96,105,2,3,8
01/01/2014,Roy Bennett,Caleb Tucker,42,17,1,5,77,92,94,92,3,1,7
01/01/2014 Christina Walker Caleb Tucker 4 8 1 4 82 06 07 06 2 2 8
```

Figure 5.8 Daily summary activity logs - formatted

Column#1	Column#2	Column#3	Column#4	Column#5	Column#6	Column#7	Column#8	Column#9
Date	Call Advisor	Team Advisor	Call Offered (Vol)	Avg HT (Min)	Call Rating (1-5)	Blocking Rate (%)	Service Level (%)	Utilization (%)
01/01/2014	Patricia King	Paul Dean	5	3	5	4	77	96
01/01/2014	Clarence Young	Roy Robbins	42	12	4	3	85	90
01/01/2014	Eugene Barnes	Pam Lowe	20	14	2	1	82	92
01/01/2014	Mildred Torres	Linda Carter	35	7	5	4	89	97
01/01/2014	Henry Wilson	Lena Roberts	39	5	1	5	93	92
01/01/2014	Eric Thomas	Alyssa Hogan	30	17	3	3	85	89
01/01/2014	Stephanie Rivera	Antonia Lamb	23	17	2	0	75	94
01/01/2014	Scott Henderson	Carol Neal	35	5	2	5	94	91
01/01/2014	Shirley Powell	Faye Patton	40	14	4	3	77	89

Business and service metrics that are fed to the capacity management tool can be sourced from various sources:

- Web log: parsing the logs can provide very useful data
- Custom Application Log
- Database : Query can be used to extract needed business and service metrics
- Data warehouse - ETL and BI tools: these are good sources for accessing business metrics for capacity planning. Examples are Business Object, Splunk, and Qlikview. Care should be exercised to ensure private and sensitive data are not extracted.
- Capacity management embedded with ETL and BI tools: some capacity management tools come with the ETL & BI functionalities, providing seamless data integration for capacity planning reporting and modelling e.g. UnlimitedAnalytics Software - data analytics & capacity management application.

BUSINESS METRICS DATA COLLECTION FORMAT

Custom business metrics can be collected and stored in data file or database. The commonly used data format for capacity data is the CSV format, but must not necessarily be comma delimited.

The delimiter can be any character; however, it is good to use a character that is hardly or never used within your metrics data stream. In some cases, the ability of a capacity management application to be able to apply more than one delimiter character within a record/metric stream is a good-to-have feature.

Typically, a data point record in metric log can be formatted using any of these record structures (the fields can be in any order), below:

Collection Timestamp, Metric-Name-UID, Measurement
Collection Timestamp, Metric-Name-UID, Measurement Value, Capacity Value

It important to note that the record structure specified above may be presented alongside other information in the file, or using other format like XML, DSV, and custom format. The tool of choice should be able to parse any data-string to extract the required fields. Furthermore, this functionality of the capacity tool, being able to extract data from logs irrespective of data structure and format will help ensure that applications' logs can be used as generated, without reformatting before feeding to CDB. In addition, the capacity tool should be able to support multiple delimiters, and more than one character delimiter.

Each of the fields with a business metric record will be described further in detail in Table 5.9.

Table 5.9   Business Metrics Record & Fields Format

Field Name	Field Description
Collection Timestamp	Use this field to track the time the measurement/data point was collected, not when it is being written to log. Different applications may have their timestamp in different formats: Unix Epoch, YYYY/MM/DD HH:NN:SS, D/M/YY H:N:S, H:N:S MM/DD/YYYY, within your capacity tool, they should be written using a common format. For example, YYYYMMDDHHNNSS, this makes it easy to query your data-date as numeric data, which is easier to manipulate.

Table 5.9 (continued)

Field Name	Field Description
	The date and time data can be split and stored using different fields, but this generally depends on what features/options your capacity tool supports.

Consolidated versus Country Peaks

For capacity planning purposes, the peak throughput rate is vital; hence, it is important that the time part (seconds, minutes, hours) of the collection timestamp is included.

Care must be taken if you have N-tier client server application where different components (e.g. web server) are hosted in different countries. In multiple time zone scenarios like this, there are two daily business and service metrics, namely:

1. Host country total volume and peak throughput
2. Global or consolidated total volume and peak throughput

The collection-timestamp of the host country log files will be based on the local time in the log. However, to get the daily consolidated/global volume or peak, this process can be used:

- Decide the common time-zone that will be used as the organization's reporting time-zone (usually, the time-zone of the headquarter country is used as the reporting-time-zone)

- Using your capacity tool, the country log's local time should be converted to the organization's defined

Table 5.9   (continued)

Field Name	Field Description

reporting-time-zone; before writing the metrics to the capacity database. For example, if the country's local time is 3 hours after GMT, and the common reporting-time-zone is 2 hours before GMT. The local country log's time for consolidated will be:

"New Country-log-time" = "Collection-country-log-time" -5 hours.

> **Success Hint:**
> To build accurate capacity planning models, it is good practice to collect both the business volume metric, service performance (throughput, and latency), and infrastructure resource usage metrics using the same sampling time interval.

Metric-Name-UID — Use this field to capture the name and paths of the metric to be measured, which is to be written to the log. Each of the metric-names to be measured and written to the log file should be unique; and so, each metric-name is seen as unique identifier (UID).

As good practice, the Metric-Name-UID should be inclusive of the unit-of-measurement (UOM) of the metric. A metric not linked with any UOM is as good as useless. For example, the metric-name-UIDs: "Daily Total Sales (Count of Sales)", "Daily Peak Sales (Sales count/minute)", and "Execution Time (seconds)", in each case the UOM is enclosed in bracket.

Table 5.9   (continued)

Field Name	Field Description

Scope of Metric-Name-UID

The Metric-Name-UID must not be used to represent a single field. Nevertheless , depending on the capacity management tool in use, the "Metric-Name-UID" can be broken into multiple fields to represent the detail path of the metric-name, using the base "Orders (count/min)":

- Instance1/Orders (count/min)
- Instance2_Orders (count/min)
- Instance2_Average Response Time (ms)
- Channel1/Orders (count/min)
- Business Group/Department/Orders (count/min)
- EMEA/Store/Orders (count/min)
- EMEA/England/Orders (count/min)
- England/London/Orders (count/min)
- England/Wales/Web/Orders (count/min)
- England/Scotland/IVR/Orders (count/min)
- England/NIreland/IVR/1-min Average Latency (ms)

Depending on the ability of your capacity tool, each of the path elements can be stored in a field, in the capacity database. This will make it possible for path specific historical metrics to be queried, and reported on; such will provide excellent data for capacity planning model where the transactions breakdown mix is vital.

Table 5.9   (continued)

Field Name	Field Description
Measurement Value	This is the numeric point in time value; measured, or aggregated value of an interval.
Capacity Value	Optionally, the capacity limit of the metric can be provided along for each metric record. The main problem with including the capacity value is that, any time the capacity value changes, the production environment script producing the data will need to be updated through the change management process.

DETERMINING BUSINESS METRIC CAPACITY LIMIT & SLA

The maximum capacity limit is the accepted measurement limit above which the measurement is considered to constitute a capacity or performance risk, capable of causing service degradation or failure.

For infrastructure or computing resources, it is much easier to know the maximum capacity limit, as these are usually specified. However, there can be additional technical specification of maximum utilization; at which the stability of a resource cannot be guaranteed. For example, if the utilization of a network device has technical utilization limit of 50% - in this case your maximum utilization capacity is 50%. Hence, for the purpose of capacity management, a raw usage value of 10% and 40%, in reality translates to effective utilization of 20%, and 80% respectively.

Infrastructure resource metrics are commonly associated with a known maximum capacity limit. However, for business and service metrics, there is no simple method for accurately determining the maximum throughput limit, above which service performance degradation or failure will set in; leading to SLA violation. Nonetheless, application performance testing, analytical modelling, etc provide means to determine the maximum service throughput, concurrency, etc. that an application can support; and also to reveal the underlying resource bottlenecks, that are responsible for the performance degradation.

Success Hint:

There can be no realistic and accurate capacity planning for future business demand; if an application's maximum service throughput (capacity limit) is not known.

PERFORMANCE TESTING

Application performance testing is a general term used in referring to different types of performance related testing with a view to determining its responsiveness, stability, and scalability characteristics under increasing workload. One of the main objectives of this test is to determine how well the SLA (e.g. response times) is complied with; under increasing demand throughput/workload, and the resultant resource utilization increase of the underlying infrastructure.

Performance testing is predominantly targeted towards application's concurrency (e.g. requests queue) characterized by soft-capacity limit. On the other hand, persistence and content capacity-request types with hard-capacity limit should also be tested.

Empathically, capacity management should be embedded in every phase of the SDLC; specifically, performance testing objectives in view of capacity management are:

- To assist the capacity management team to determine the maximum business volume/service throughput an application can handle without breaching SLA performance target, in terms of latency, response time, etc. This maximum service throughput value, obtained from performance testing, becomes the focal point when building capacity planning model to determine the infrastructure resource needed to support future business demand, and its associated service throughput.

- Helps to uncover infrastructure and computing resources (e.g. utilization of CPU, memory, network, input-output, etc.) that will constitute performance bottleneck under sustained high service throughput, and user load. Consequently, the current hardware and application configuration helps to determine the realistic maximum utilization level an infrastructure or computing resource can be driven to. This also provides the right basis to set the appropriate threshold alerting against infrastructure or computing resources.

- Aids in determining application's scalability, and its scaling methods:

  o Vertical (scaling up) – increasing or adding resources to the existing hardware. For example, replacing the server CPU cores with a faster one, or with more CPUs; adding more memory, etc. This scaling method is dependent on the application, and operating ability to use the added resources.

  o Horizontal (scaling out) – increasing infrastructure or computing resource by adding new nodes (sets of servers working together to deliver service) to the existing ones. This will be useful for applications that run on multiples nodes, using a load balancer to route the workload traffic between the nodes.

Success Hint:

It is good to use the same monitoring tools in both the production and performance testing environments.

PERFORMANCE TESTING TYPES

The term performance testing encompasses different types of tests, comprising of: load testing, stress testing, soak testing, and single thread workload testing. Table 5.10, provides a comparative review of the types. You need to choose the most suitable for your application.

Table 5.10   Performance Tests Types Compared

Performance Test Type	Test Description
Load Testing	• This test is aimed at determining the upper limit of capacity that a system can withstand before SLA is breached. • Prior to the application's breaking point (before the performance requirements breach occurs), the infrastructure or computing resources constituting performance bottleneck can be identified, and the maximum utilization noted. In addition, the maximum business and service throughput should also be noted.

Table 5.10 (continued)

Performance Test Type	Test Description
	• Hence, the expected key measurements from this test are: service throughput rates, latency, and infrastructure resource utilization. The combination of the information obtained from this test, the historical metrics data, and the future business demand are used as input into the capacity modelling tool towards predicting the future service performance, and resource capacity needs.
	• To ensure this test provides useful result, the test load mix should be close to production load obtained through workload characterization, and same applies to the load arrival rate.
	• It is used for identifying application, computing, and infrastructure limitations/bottlenecks that are not visible through statistical modelling
Stress Testing	• This test is similar to load testing, but focuses on determining how the application will respond if the load is above the expected maximum.
	• It further serves to identify application bugs that arise due to high load conditions e.g. memory leaks.
Soak Testing	• This test is also known as endurance testing, and is aimed at

Table 5.10   (continued)

Performance Test Type	Test Description
	determining how an application will respond, under sustained load above the maximum. In reality, sustained load is what gives rise to capacity risk; hence, it is good to consider how the performance of your application will be impacted if 50% of the daily load comes within an hour.
Single Thread Workload Testing	• This test is targeted at determining the resource cost of a single business workload or function running alone on the server. • The key objective is to determine the resource cost - service time (the amount of time spent in using a single infrastructure or computing resource; when a single transaction is the workload). For example, the test can provide the number of CPU seconds the server uses in processing a single technical transaction. • This performance test type is a key input in building analytical model, which is used for resource utilization forecasting. This implies that a single thread workload testing used with analytical queuing network model; can be used to determine resource capacity limit, consequently eliminating the need for expensive load/stress testing.

SUMMARY

Accurate and reliable capacity planning will almost be impossible using infrastructure resource metrics only; instead, capacity planning should be based on the business capacity-driving metrics that drives infrastructure resource utilization. Regrettably, most vendor monitoring tools do not focus on the collection of these, as there are no standard techniques for their collection. The instrumentation methods and extraction processes vary, and are highly customized for each application.

The business metrics collected should include the volumetric and performance (throughput and latency) measurements, these remain the most appropriate way to measure how well the provided IT service is received by the users (human or other dependent IT systems), and provides the basis for SLA with the business. Business metric instrumentation is best built into the application at the early stage of SDLC. The instrumentation can be implemented as time stamped activity logs.

For the business metrics monitoring to be meaningful for capacity management, the maximum throughput the application can sustain for a given business metric, without performance degradation or SLA violation, should be known. The throughput capacity can be determined by performance testing or statistical modelling; however, the infrastructure and computing resources causing performance bottleneck cannot be exposed using statistical modelling.

ORGANIZATIONAL APPRAISAL

1. Besides system resource metrics utilization, do you have any process in place for collecting business performance metrics (business activity throughput - the actual driver of system resource utilization; and latency)?
2. Is your organization's formal capacity management report meant for senior management and regulators based on only the principal business metrics?

3. For your IT services, do you capture the business performance metrics (throughput and latency) at the appropriate peak second/minute/hour of the day?

4. In determining the capacity limit of your principal business metrics, is performance testing or other reliable methods employed?

5. Are the principal business metrics for each IT system determined using the "question and answer" technique outlined earlier in this chapter?

6 DATA AGGREGATION METHODS & GRANULARITY

"Details create the big picture"

- Sanford I. Weill.

INTRODUCTION

Data aggregation is a technique of summarizing the numerous data points collected against a specific capacity driver. The aggregated value of a metric is the single value that can be used in reporting capacity and other capacity related functions like modelling. For example, if a monitoring tool collects a specific metric every 5 seconds, then, in a day it would have collected 21600 data points. However, with data aggregation you can have one aggregated value for each day or hour.

DATA AGGREGATION METHODS

With respect to capacity management, there are different data aggregation functions, or methods that can be applied to periodic data points to get the single data point that will be used in capacity management's functions – analysis, reporting, modelling, etc.

The data aggregation method you choose will determine the outputs you get from your capacity management process and the resultant decisions you make. Consequently, specific aggregation method adopted for a process should be aligned to the characteristics of the data set.

While choosing a monitoring tool or developing one in-house, it is important to ensure that several data aggregation methods are supported.

Figure 6.1, elucidates the graphical comparison of different aggregation methods for the same data set; the computed aggregated values are shown by indicated lines.

Figure 6.1 Data Aggregation Methods Graphical Comparison

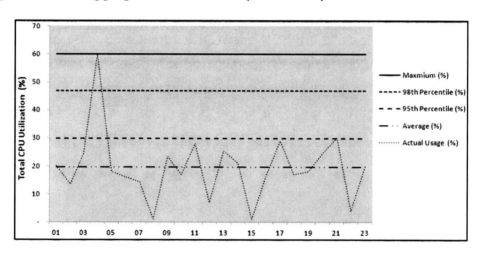

The different aggregation methods have their unique characteristics and use cases, particularly as it affects the three capacity-request types – concurrency, persistence, and content capacity-request types. The aggregation methods include: sum, average, median, minimum, maximum, percentile, and all-time-high (ATH). Table 6.2, outlines some key advantages and disadvantages of each, and their likely use cases.

Table 6.2 (continued) Data Aggregation Methods Compared

Method Name	Advantages	Disadvantages
Sum/Total	• Good for business volumetric metrics, as business user can relate it to their demand forecasting, based on periodic sum/total. "Daily Active Users" is an example. • A must have aggregation method; when determining the capacity requirement for persistence, and content capacity-request types.	Not good for concurrency capacity-request type metrics.
Average[1]	• It provides an indication of how busy a resource was, over a period of time. • For evenly distributed utilization, period average can be used to detect abnormal trend that is of interest in capacity management. It is good for alerting unexpected	Obscures the troughs in dataset, can lead to infrastructure under provisioning; and resultant capacity risk. Not good enough to be used in capacity planning model as the focus should be on peak utilization.

Table 6.2 (continued) Data Aggregation Methods Compared

Method Name	Advantages	Disadvantages
	deviations from baseline.	
Median	• Provides a more realistic value for determining the middle value from a metric dataset.	Not good enough to be used in capacity planning model as the focus should be on peak utilization.
	• Does not get obscured by either very large or very low values.	
Minimum	• Required when measurement provides resource availability rather than utilization. Point of minimum resource availability, is of importance for capacity management.	Not a popular aggregation method in capacity management as the process focuses on peak values.
Maximum	• Maximum value is good for aggregating Business volumetric and throughputs.	Maximum aggregation method is not ideal for infrastructure resource metrics, as it can lead to infrastructure over provisioning.

Table 6.2 (continued) Data Aggregation Methods Compared

Method Name	Advantages	Disadvantages
	• Good for tracking the periodic peak value, irrespective of the duration.	Any spike in utilization over the monitored period, is taken as the period maximum. The maximum can be unrealistic, as it can be related to system booting process.
	• For root cause analysis, single spike in utilization becomes the maximum usage over the monitored period and can be a useful clue in indentifying incident root cause.	Capacity management focuses on sustained load or usage, rather than non recurring spikes.
Percentile	• Percentile aggregation can be applied if the absolute peak of a dataset is to be ignored. Hence, it is good for aggregating infrastructure resource usage, or business metrics throughput datasets where there is need to eliminate non-sustained	Percentile aggregation functionality is not often provided in both proprietary and open source monitoring tools - due to the resource intensiveness required for the calculation. Some tools provide apparent (line indication on display screen)

Table 6.2 (continued) Data Aggregation Methods Compared

Method Name	Advantages	Disadvantages
	spikes.	percentile functionality, without any associated data that can be used for further analysis in capacity planning models.
	• The percentile factor to be used depends on the spike threshold to be excluded and the volume of data over the aggregation time window.	For in-house tool development, Microsoft Excel provides this functionality.
	• 95th, 98th, and 99th percentile factors are more popular for concurrency capacity-request types; however, analyzing the sample data using various percentile factors and comparing same with the maximum value can be used to decide the more suitable factor. In reality, it is good to have aggregated data based on	An approximate percentile value can be calculated using simple logic. For example, to calculate the estimated N^{th} percentile value for any dataset, here are the steps (assume $N^{th} = 95^{th}$): 1) Sort the dataset values in ascending order - from lowest to highest 2) Count the number of values within the dataset

Table 6.2 (continued) Data Aggregation Methods Compared

Method Name	Advantages	Disadvantages
	two or more percentile factors; as this will increase the chances of finding better correlation with other metrics when using the trending or analytical modelling.	(assume it is N), then compute 100%-95% (5%), of the dataset count (assume K = N x 5/100) ; 3) Using the ordered list obtained in #1, from the entry of the list, move K places down, the next value of the ordered list is the approximate 95th percentile value of the dataset.
All-Time-High (ATH)	• ATH is the highest ever value of a particular metrics. Serves as reference point for comparative reporting. • Good reference point for capacity planning decisions regarding scaling up, or downsizing the application's infrastructure	May not be available in commercial capacity tools; and sometimes difficult to maintain. Can be misleading as it is only of historical importance, and not a good pointer to the future

[1] In all cases skip nil, null and zero measurements (except where zero is an expected measurement from data source) as such will distort the result obtained for any calculated aggregation methods like average, and percentile. This can be avoided, if you limit data collection to only the trading hours.

DERIVED METRICS

It is possible to come across some monitoring tool providing resource usage measurements that may not be suitable in capacity report. A typical case is where a monitoring provides the "Memory Available (%)" metric, rather than "Memory Used (%)" metric.

The focus of capacity management is resource utilization, so it makes more sense to derive "utilization (%)" from "availability %" using the formula:

Memory Used (%) = 100 – Memory Available (%)

The "Memory Used (%)" metric above is called derived metrics, like other conventional usage based metrics; it provides usage value that can be subjected to a standard threshold alerting band.

Sometimes, you may not have the luxury of having data stored for the various aggregation methods. In such situation, you will need to derive the unknown aggregation value from the known value by applying a known ratio.

For example, you may be monitoring a system that provides only daily average values, but what you actually need is the daily peak values for your capacity management decision or planning model. To get the daily peak, you need to scale daily average using the baseline peak-to-average ratio.

Peak Value = Average value x peak-to-average-ratio

The baseline peak-to-average-ratio needs to be recalculated often, to ensure the value reflects the current usage trend.

DATA AGGREGATION GRANULARITY/RESOLUTION

Metrics collection or aggregation resolution determines the level of granularity or time interval at which measurement data can be collected and aggregated before using them for capacity planning decision.

No single data resolution/time interval is ideal for all data providers; different data provider or source will be measured using different time intervals that best suits the data characteristics.

The lower the collection resolution or granularity, the more work load the instrumentation will add to the target application providing the data. Thus, the use of lower collection resolution should be justified. Monitoring should not contribute to performance issue; in practice, the metrics collection should not consume more than 1% of the system resources.

Table 6.3 is a list of some common measurement resolutions, and their likely use cases. Howbeit, in reality the data source type, and the application of the data will determine the ideal resolution or granularity to be applied for aggregation. Whilst choosing a monitoring tool or developing one in-house, it is important to ensure that it supports data aggregation at various granularity levels. The common data aggregation resolution or granularity types are: second, minute, hour, day, week, month, quarter, and year.

Table 6.3 Data granularity considerations

Granularity	Consideration & Use Cases
Second	• The second granularity data finds use where spike in usage can

Table 6.3 (continued)

Granularity	Consideration & Use Cases
	impact service performance, or is valuable for detailed performance analysis. This is useful for systems that expose resource usage like CPU load; and very high user activities platform, like ecommerce, financial trading, telecommunications, etc. • Measurement collected every N [1] seconds, or aggregated over N seconds. • Capacity planning modelling is best based on metrics usage over the one second peak window [2].
Minute	• Measuring user activities or work load of an application
Hourly	• For daily report breakdown
Daily	• For weekly and monthly report breakdown. • Good for modelling and forecasting resource usage.
Weekly	• Weekly average aggregation can be very good for spotting unusual weekly trends.
Monthly	• For historical and comparative reporting. • Good for capacity plan supporting reports.
Quarterly	• Simple and concise reporting for senior managers.

Table 6.3 (continued)

Granularity	Consideration & Use Cases
Yearly	• For year by year comparative reporting.

[1] N is a representation of any number for example 1, 2, 20, etc.

[2] This will be discussed further in the "Modelling & Resource Forecasting" section of the "Capacity planning" chapter.

SUMMARY

Data plays prominent role in capacity management, and its importance cannot be over emphasized. The quality of insight provided by data depends so much on:

- The granularity level at which the data is initially collected
- The granularity level at which the data is aggregated
- The aggregation method used

The maximum and average aggregation methods, if not properly used can lead to infrastructure over or under provisioning respectively. Nevertheless, the maximum aggregation method can be used in incident investigation, and root cause analysis; while the average aggregation method can be used to determine busy level or load distribution.

For system resource metrics, the percentile based aggregation method is more ideal for capacity planning, as it can be used to eliminate one-off spikes, and focus on sustained peaks. Disappointingly, a good number of commercial monitoring tools do not provide real and flexible percentile aggregation functionality.

ORGANIZATIONAL APPRAISAL

1. In calculating system resource summary/aggregation, is the percentile aggregation method employed? The percentile aggregation removes the effect of noise, spikes, and troughs in the dataset – which average and maximum aggregation methods do not

2. Does the vendor- implemented monitoring tools for your organization, support the invaluable percentile aggregation method?

7 CAPACITY DATABASE (CDB) & DATA STORAGE TECHNIQUES

"If you only have a hammer, you tend to see every problem as a nail"

- Abraham Maslow

INTRODUCTION

Capacity management depends essentially on collecting and analyzing data. Therefore, the process, success will depend largely on properly storing the data, and the ease of accessing, analyzing, reporting and extracting the data. The data storage component of the capacity management process system tool is identified by different names, amongst them are: Capacity Database (CDB), or Capacity Information management System (CMIS); we use the name tagged as CDB.

The method adopted in storing the metrics in the database plays a vital role in the usability, reliability, reporting flexibility, and scalability of the CDB system.

For organizations that choose to implement a commercial / third party solution, this may not be given serious attention; conversely, the reverse is the case for organizations building, and implementing an in-house solution.

IMPLEMENTING CAPACITY DATABASE (CDB/CMIS)

The Capacity Database (CDB) is an ITIL version 2 (in ITIL version 3, it is called capacity Management information System (CMIS)) term used to describe the data repository that holds capacity management process data. It includes but is not limited to business, service, and resources actual metrics from IT services in scope. Also stored in CDB are: metrics capacity limit, SLA, metrics' alert usage threshold, business forecast data, and modelling parameters.

Even though CDB by nomenclature is referred to as "database", it is just a repository which can be implemented using a relational database system (RDBMS), spreadsheet, no-SQL database, etc. Irrespective of the implementation, minimally, it should be able to support the generation of desired capacity reports by users. Figure 7.1, shows some components of the capacity management process model that can be embedded or implemented within a typical CDB.

Figure 7.1 Components of CDB / CMIS

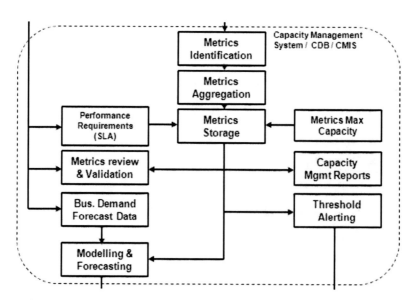

For a base CDB system, the "Metrics Storage" functionality is pivotal, and the key input is the uniquely identified and mapped business, service, and resource metrics; while the minimum output is "Capacity Management reports". However, if proactive capacity planning is to happen, all CDB functionalities shown in Figure 7.1 and more are expected to be provided by a CDB system. Each component of CDB shown in Figure 7.1 is further discussed in other chapters.

CDB DATA AGGREGATION IMPLEMENTATTION STRATEGY: HARD VS SOFT

Usually, capacity management decisions are made using the aggregated values from data collected over a period of time. Such aggregated data are fed into the reporting, modelling, and alerting mechanism of the process.

The aggregated data can be generated and maintained in a CDB using any of the following techniques:

1. **Hard Aggregation**: Compute and store (all aggregated values are stored in the CDB)
2. **Soft Aggregation**: Full dynamic compute (No aggregated value is stored in the CDB)
3. Using the combination of both hard and soft techniques (some aggregated values are stored in the CDB)

For example: An application generates its trading log (containing timestamp, and number of transactions traded every second) , and the log is fed into CDB. The typical daily data points are analyzed thus:

a) Based on the per second log data for each day, a total of 86400 transactional metric data points / records will be stored in CDB repository

b) The typical aggregated data points available for the scenario above can be illustrated using Figure 7.2 (three aggregation types - sum, maximum, and average; and four granularity levels - second, minute, hour, and day). The aggregated values can be made available to users using either hard or soft method.

Figure 7.2 Typical aggregated data points daily summary for a single

Data points per day	Sum of Transaction	Maximum of Transaction	Average of Transactions
Second	86400	86400	86400
Minute	1440	1440	1440
Hourly	24	24	24
Daily	1	1	1

- Hard Aggregation (Compute and Store): at end of the day, for each of the three aggregation types (sum, maximum, and average) the CDB will compute and store 86400, 1440, 24, 1 data points for the second, minute, hour, and daily granularity respectively - as shown in Figure 7.2. Once the aggregated data is stored, then the raw dataset (stored in the CDB) can be deleted

- Soft Aggregation (Full Dynamic): aggregated data will be not be computed, nor stored; but, will be computed on demand as long as the raw dataset (stored in the CDB @ #a above) is available

- Partial Dynamic: In this case, the aggregated value will be computed and stored for one or more (but not all) of the granularity levels, while the

102

aggregated values of higher order granularity levels are derived from the stored data. For example, if the hourly aggregated metrics are stored; when required, the daily can be dynamically computed for any date using stored hourly.

Each approach has its own advantages, and challenges. Table 7.3, compares the hard and soft aggregation implementation strategies. The choice between these two should be carefully made based on business environment, size of IT estate and the overall CDB design approach.

Table 7.3   Hard vs. Soft Aggregation Techniques Compared

Feature	Hard Aggregation	Soft Aggregation
Storage types	The aggregated values are computed and stored in the repository for each of the granularity levels and aggregation methods[1] during periodic CDB update process.	Aggregated values are neither computed nor stored in CDB by the periodic update process; but the desired aggregated values are dynamically computed and used on demand.
Storage Space consumed	A lot of storage space is required; as both the raw and all aggregated data are stored.	Minimal storage space is required as only raw data is stored.
Storage interval	Aggregated values are computed and stored in the repository, at	Only the raw data are stored as they become available; either as near real-time or scheduled

Table 7.3   (continued)

Feature	Hard Aggregation	Soft Aggregation
	designated interval as part of the periodic hourly / daily / weekly / monthly process run.	process.
Aggregated data availability	Aggregated data are not immediately available for use, until the periodic aggregation run. Thus, it may not be good for intraday or real-time dashboard / reporting.	Aggregated data is available always as long as the dependent low granular data is available. The implication is that the dynamically computed aggregation value is bound to change if the dependent data source changes. This is ideal where intraday metrics values are required
System Resource Overhead	Aggregated data retrieval has minimal resource overhead on the repository system.	Aggregated data retrieval has more resource overhead on the repository system.
Reliability	The aggregated data reliability depends on the accuracy and the success rate of the calculations, and also of the scheduled batch job designed to compute the aggregated	Dynamically computed aggregated values can be more reliable; and more easily verified.

Table 7.3   (continued)

Feature	Hard Aggregation	Soft Aggregation
	values.	
End-user Satisfaction	Report generation based on already stored aggregated values are faster, and provides better end-user satisfaction.	Dynamically computed aggregation transfers the time costs to the end-users, hence, report generation is slower.
Ease of changes	Changes to aggregation calculations or formulae will affect already stored data. Thus, can lead to aggregated data reloading.	Calculation changes do not affect any stored data.
Raw Data Retention & Stripping	Raw data can be stripped without affecting the already computed aggregated data.	Stripping the raw data impacts the aggregated data; for period the raw data is stripped/deleted, aggregated data will no longer be available.
Technical Implementation	It is more difficult to maintain the aggregated values. Besides, the ability to undo prior data loading (and restore prior aggregated values) is a	Easier to implement, as computed aggregated value does not need to be stored or maintained.

Table 7.3   (continued)

Feature	Hard Aggregation	Soft Aggregation
	desired feature.	

[1] Avoid storing average values as they pose a lot of problems maintaining their values, rather store and maintain "Sum" and "Count" aggregated values and use them to compute average value when required.

Success Hint:

For high volume data systems, performance is gained when intraday average values are computed from periodically stored "Sum" and "Count" aggregated values.

CDB DATA REPOSITORY IMPLEMENTATION STRATEGY: SEPARATE VS. COMBINED

In designing a CDB system, consideration should be given to the appropriate repository technique that will be used to store the metrics data from the different IT services. This consideration is driven by:

- The number of IT services within the organization to be hosted in the CDB
- The frequency of metrics data upload to the CDB
- The volume of data coming from each IT service
- The scalability of the CDB system

There are mainly two types of metrics storage techniques that can be adopted for storing each IT service in a CDB; these are:

1. Separate metrics repository per IT service

2. Combined metrics repository for all IT services

The "Separate metrics repository per IT service" repository type can further be separated into different repository types based on the data granularity (aggregation period). This means that the repositories can be split into raw (none aggregated), minute, hour, day, week, month, quarter, and year respectively, depending on what is applicable for the CDB. The comparison between the two types of repository is shown in Table 7.4.

Table 7.4   Metrics Repository Implementation Types

Feature	Separate Repository	Combined Repository
Database Design Concept	• Each IT service is identified with a unique identifier number (UID); the UID can be the organization's unique IT system asset number. The UID is added to the data tables associated with it either as prefix or suffix. For example, an IT system with UID of 741, can have a table named "history_data_741" to hold its historical metrics. The base table name is "history_data".	Metrics data from all IT services are held in a single repository.
	• The repository separation at	Metrics data for aggregation

Table 7.4   (continued)

Feature	Separate Repository	Combined Repository
	data granularity or aggregation level can also be applied. For the case above, the tables can be named thus: "history_data_hour_741", "history_data_day_741", etc. The base table names are "history_data_hour" and "history_data_day" respectively. •	levels are held in a single repository.
Meta Data Navigation	• Meta data control is required to help navigate users to the repository/table that corresponds with the user desired IT service/aggregation level.	No meta data control is required.
Scalability	• Very ideal for growth scaling	May not be able to scale out for growth
Query Performance	• Provides good response time for end-users	As the data volume grows, data retrieval may face performance degradation.

Table 7.4 (continued)

Feature	Separate Repository	Combined Repository

SUMMARY

The capacity database (CDB), also called capacity management information system (CMIS), is a key component of the capacity management process. It is a data repository that holds the actual measurement data, collected from the business, service, and resource sub processes. In addition, it can be used for metrics capacity limit, SLA, threshold alert values, business forecast data, and modelling parameters storage.

Even though the capacity database is entitled "database", in reality, it is just a repository which can be implemented using a relational database system (RDBMS), spreadsheet, no-SQL database, etc. Irrespective of the implementation, minimally, it should be able to support the generation of desired capacity reports by users.

Some third party monitoring tools come embedded with CDB/CMIS components; on the other hand, it can also be implemented in-house, though not recommended for organizations with large IT estate. However, if it must be implemented in-house using RDBMS, the design should ensure that data extraction and capacity report generation is within an acceptable response time; in both real-time and historical mode. It is recommended that the CDB application/database designer, choose between:

- The hard versus soft data aggregation techniques;
- The separate versus combined data repository implementation techniques.

ORGANIZATIONAL APPRAISAL

1. Has your organization implemented any form of capacity database (CDB) for business and resource metrics collection, storage, analysis and reporting?

2. Are the lower granularity data kept long enough in the CDB, to help with problem root cause analysis before they are stripped off the database?

3. Is your CDB's data storage and aggregation strategy, carefully planned to meet performance expectation based on your IT estate size?

8 CAPACITY REPORTS

"The first step in good reporting is good snooping"

- Matt Drudge.

INTRODUCTION

The ability of the capacity management process to fulfil its core function of proactively eliminating capacity-caused service failure depends largely on the insight, robustness, timeliness, and quality of the reports produced by the process.

Unlike capacity planning report that is about future utilization, the capacity management report is about the past actual utilization and the future utilization. Capacity management reports can be operational, tactical, or strategic in nature depending on the target audience.

The capacity management report should include details of both the current business volumetric, service performance and infrastructure resources utilization.

Some of the basic standard required of capacity management reports are:

- Ad-hoc capacity reporting - both business and technical users should be able to compose and generate desired chart based reports, with options of being able to view reporting using different chart types
- Periodic standard reports should be automated, and automatically delivered to need-to-know audience, and should be scheduled based on reporting interval agreed with the users/business
- Reports should be chart based, as visual conveys information faster than textual reports, except for listing-confined report e.g. Top N server with the highest CPU utilization

CAPACITY REPORTS TYPES BY AUDIENCE

Table 8.1, shows typical capacity managements report audience, and the report types that will provide them useful information towards proactive capacity management. The report is based on the aggregated metrics across all the 3 sub processes - business, service, and resource. Typically, the capacity management report audience includes: capacity management leads, IT service owners, IT service managers, business managers, risk managers, application support, external regulators, etc.

Success Hint:

Any capacity report produced and meant for stakeholders should be able to provide input for operational, tactical, or strategic decision making; else, it should be stopped.

The objective of having different audiences for capacity management report is to drive users and management support for the process, and to show how it is adding value to the organization. It also gives the process visibility within the organization, and draws attention to capacity risks yet to be managed.

Table 8.1   Capacity Reports, Audience and Frequency

Report Audience	Report Description, Ownership & Responsibilities	Frequency
Capacity Analysts	• Owns and reviews all reports (automated and scheduled). Further analyses and escalates red threshold breaches to capacity management leads.	Daily
Capacity Management Leads	• Review and follow up reports for the audience of system owners and senior managers. Initiate infrastructure capacity scale up/down with IT service owners.	Daily/ Weekly

Application Support	• Report focus & listings - Reports based on weekly peak/maximum capacity utilization:
	
	   o All metrics with usage that breached SLA, or specified Red threshold
	   o All other metrics with capacity utilization exceeding 90%
	   o All metrics of content or persistence capacity type e.g. storage having 30 or less days to full capacity (DTFC)
	   o All metrics recording new highest capacity utilization, or all time high
		Weekly

113

Table 8.1 (continued)

Report Audience	Report Description, Ownership & Responsibilities	Frequency
	value (ATH)	
	o For each metrics category, Top N^1 metrics in capacity utilization	
	o For each metrics category, bottom N^1 metrics in capacity utilization	
	o Resources with the N^1 lowest all-time-high (ATH) usage are good candidate for downsizing (exclude active-passive clusters)	
IT Service Owners, and Service Managers	• Report focus & listings - Business, and service capacity reports based on monthly peak measurement, are grouped by department/IT applications:	Monthly
	o All business and service metrics with usage that breached SLA target, or other specified threshold	
	o All other business and service capacity metrics with capacity utilization exceeding 90%	
	o All business and service metrics recording new all time high value (ATH)	
	o Top N^1 IT services/applications with highest business and service capacity	

Table 8.1 (continued)

Report Audience	Report Description, Ownership & Responsibilities	Frequency
	utilization.	
	o Bottom N^1 IT services/applications with lowest business and service capacity utilization.	
	o Monthly business capacity summary report, with emphasis on the historical trend, forecast volume, and service incidents attributed to inadequate capacity.	
Senior business & risk managers	• Executive capacity management macro and high-level report, with one chart each to highlights the capacity status of each business group, region, division, etc. Characteristically, the report is business capacity focused, and should provide the following information: o Actual: Quarterly peaks of business volume, and capacity line for the last 18-24 months o Projected business volume for the next 2 quarters, and the assurance that there is adequate capacity to cover same. o For the quarter under review, the	Quarterly

Table 8.1 (continued)

Report Audience	Report Description, Ownership & Responsibilities	Frequency
	number of medium or high service incidents with insufficient capacity as cause, and the current resolution status. ○ Status report of current, and future capacity management projects	
External Regulatory body	• In some business sectors (e.g. finance, banking, etc.), there are regulatory requirements for organizations to periodically provide their enterprise capacity management report; for the following reasons: ○ To provide assurance to the regulators that effective capacity management process is in place ○ To provide assurance to the regulators that there is adequate capacity to cope with the current and future transaction volumes.	

[1] N can be 10, but is determined by the size of the IT estate

CAPACITY REPORT - DISPLAY OPTIONS COMPARED

Capacity reports can be displayed in different forms ranging from graphic, tabular, or a combination of both. The format to be used largely depends on the audience, and the report focus.

Capacity report should dwell on used capacity, and not on availability. Capacity management reports convey quick message when both the metric's measurement value and the capacity limit of the report can be presented based on 100% utilization scale.

The importance of report format cannot be over emphasized. Thus, it is expected that the capacity management tool should allow users view the same report using various display options. Typical capacity report display options are further discussed below; among them are: scatter, heat map, line, trending, stacked column, 100% staked column, clustered column, pie, geographical, and tabular. Sample reports shown below are demo reports from UnlimitedAnalytics (a business analytics and capacity management software, created by the author).

1. **Scatter chart with linear correlation and R-squared values**
   - The scatter chart report (shown in Figure 8.2), is used to establish the relationship between two different metrics. It provides the correlation coefficient, and R-squared value between the dependent and independent variables. This is very useful for building regression model; for relating business/service data and resource utilization.

   - The R-squared value is a statistical measure of how two datasets are fitted to the regression line. The closer R^2 value is to 1.0 the better the relationship, conversely, the closer the value is to zero (0), the worse the relationship. R^2

value of 1.0 represents a perfect correlation. A positive R value means both variables are increasing in the same direction; while a negative value implies that as one variable increases, the other decreases.

- This is often used in ad-hoc reporting, to determine if metrics-pair can be used in the capacity planning model. For the capacity model to be reliable for capacity planning, R^2 value in the range of 0.80 to 1.0 should be targeted.

- This report type is best when intergraded with the capacity tool, as the capacity analyst will use it often to test metrics-pair for correlation relationship. Spreadsheet application can also be used to work out R-squared values.

- Generally, linear correlation is not ideal for infrastructure resource metrics e.g. CPU utilization, as they do not behave linearly after some threshold level.

Figure 8.2 Scatter Points Report

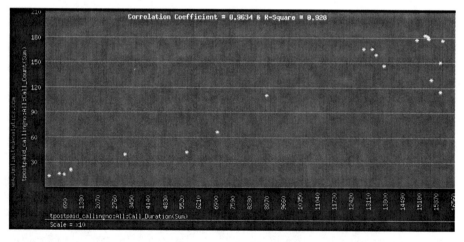

2. Heat Map Report

- The heat map report (shown in Figure 8.3a and 8.3b), is a colour-based visual representation of metric values, using colours mapped to different value ranges.

- Ideal for reports where there are many data points, which when shown using the regular chart types will be too dense and confusing.

- Also, it is ideal for conveying summary information.

Figure 8.3a Heat Map Report

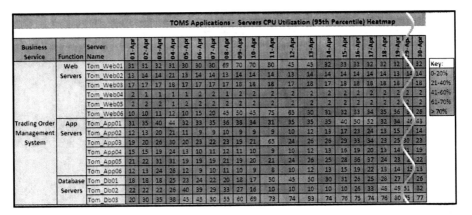

Figure 8.3b Heat Map Report

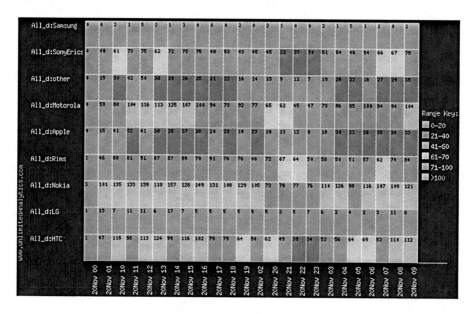

3. **Line Chart Report**

    *   The line chart report (shown in Figure 8.4a), is good for displaying historical trend for metrics with many data points

    *   Ideal for reporting detailed comparative analysis of two or more metrics

    *   It is ideal for investigating IT service performance incidents; as the spikes, peaks and troughs may be correlated with incident time.

    *   Its ability to support many data points makes it an ideal report type for correlation, linear trending, and forecasting as their accuracy depends more on larger data samples.

    *   Care should be taken in applying linear trending against historical data to forecast the future; this assumes that tomorrow will be same as yesterday, which is obviously not true.

120

- It should be known that most infrastructure resources usage e.g. 'CPU Utilization' do not behave linearly; particularly after some threshold level, consequently, it is not advisable to use trending to predict their future utilization.

- Figure 8.4b, is a single metric line-chart showing the trend line through the metric's data points, the associated correlation, and R-squared values.

- Figure 8.4c, is also a single metric line-chart showing a linear trending based forecast value, at N future periods (N is specified by user, and based on chart's unit period).

Figure 8.4a Line Chart Report

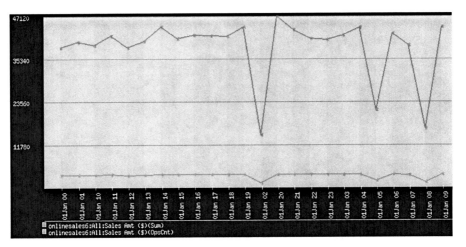

Figure 8.4b Linear Trend Line Report

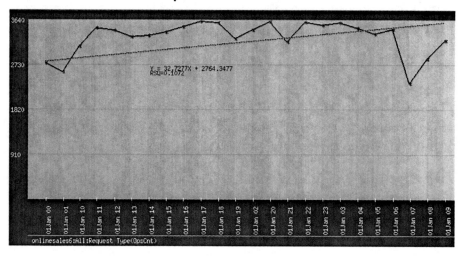

Figure 8.4c Linear Trending & Forecasting Report

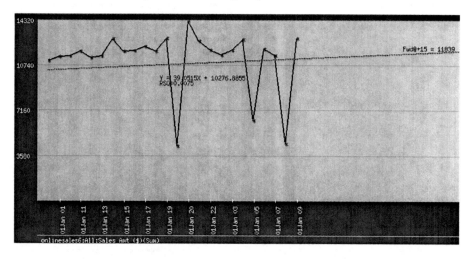

4. Stacked Column Chart Report

- The stacked column chart report (shown in Figure 8.5), is good for high level summary report, where the periodic total and individual contributions over time are required.

- Offers better view with smaller data points; thus, it is ideal for monthly or quarterly aggregated reports meant for senior business users

- Provides historical comparative view.

- Ensure that the stacked metrics have common unit of measurement, otherwise, you will be making wrong comparison.

Figure 8.5 Stacked Column Chart Report

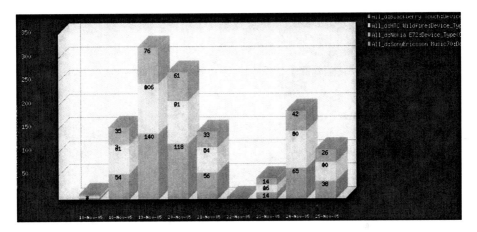

5. **100% Stacked Column Chart Report**
   - The 100% stacked column chart report (shown in Figure 8.6), is suitable for high level summary report; where the focus is to show the contribution by each individual or component members, in percentage, over a period.

   - The focus is percentage contribution of each component, and not absolute metrics values

   - Highlights the workload mix information that is useful in building capacity model, helping the business users to rightly forecast the business demand input to the capacity planning model.

- Provides better view with smaller data points, thus, it is ideal for monthly or quarterly aggregated reports meant for senior business users

- Provides comparative percentage contributions over period

- Ensures that the stacked metrics have common unit of measurement, otherwise, you will be making wrong comparison.

Figure 8.6 100% Stacked Column Chart Report

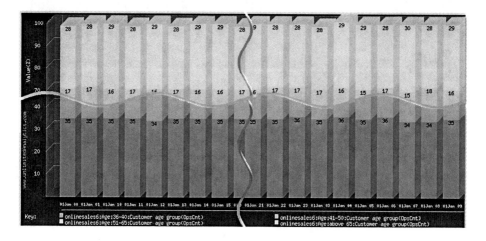

6. **Clustered Column Chart Report**
   - The 100% stacked column chart report (shown in Figure 8.7), is good for high level summary report, which focuses on comparing different metrics value, side by side over some time interval.

   - Unlike the stacked column chart, this can be used to compare metrics of different types and different units of measurement.

   - The report's focus is to show the volumetric relationship between one metric and another

- To ensure that this report type coveys clear information at a glance, it is recommended that it should have not more than 3 metrics or datasets

Figure 8.7 Clustered Column Chart Report

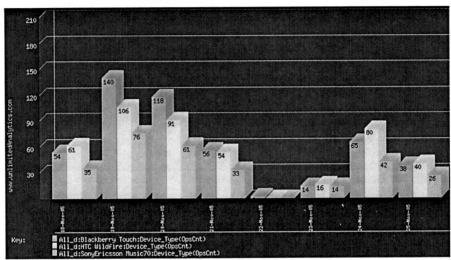

7. **Pie Chart Report**

- The pie chart report (shown in Figure 8.8a), is appropriate for presenting executive summary report, where the top/bottom N performing metrics are required. It can clearly highlight the IT services and infrastructure resource dependencies likely to cause capacity risk. Also, can highlight areas of excess capacity (over provisioning) that should be targeted for capacity reduction, towards cost savings.
- This chart report type is meant to report on only one metrics at a time.
- The report can be based on the "Top N", and "Bottom N" reporting model, shown in Figure 8.8b

125

Figure 8.8a Pie Chart Executive Summary Report

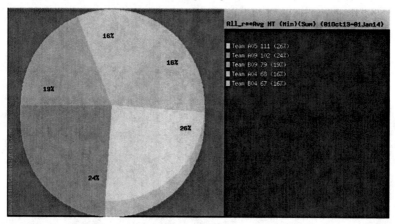

Figure 8.8b Pie Chart Report Options

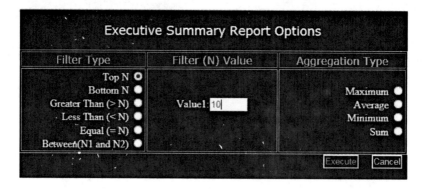

8. **Geo Chart Report**

- The geo chart report (shown in Figure 8.9), is ideal for presenting report using map visualization based on geographical location

- It is the geographical version of the heat map, but with no value range mapping to colour codes

- Will find more use in organizations that have multiple locations (county, state, country, etc.) service hosting, business transactions or presence

- Highlights capacity risk severity (using colour coding) at each location

Figure 8.9 Geo Chart Report

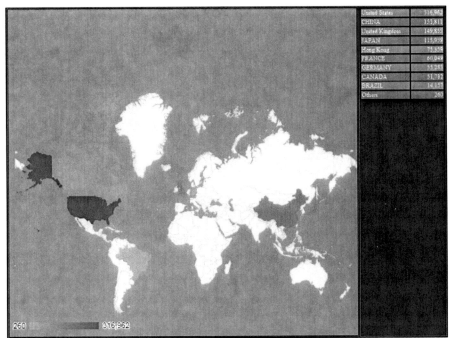

9. Tabular Report

- The tabular, non-chart based report is the conventional reporting type that comes with most capacity management tools. It can come in form of vertical and horizontal tabular reports, as shown in Figure 8.10a and Figure 8.10b.

- It is important that for all chart based reports, the user should be able to export the underlying data to text or spreadsheet document, for further analysis as desired

- In vertical tabular reports, the metrics are listed as columns, while the metric-date is listed in rows; the reverse is the case for horizontal tabular report

127

Figure 8.10a Vertical Tabular Report

Date	All_d:All:AHT Forecast Vs Actual (%)(Sum)	All_d:All:Call Offered (Vol)(Sum)	All_d:All:Blocking Rate (%)(Sum)	All_d:All:Abandoned Call (Vol)(Sum)	All_d:All:Avg HT (Min)(Sum)
01-Apr-14	3,308	706	79	66	325
02-Apr-14	9,281	1,817	242	193	948
03-Apr-14	8,727	1,708	217	145	906
04-Apr-14	8,961	2,037	262	201	1,031
05-Apr-14	8,622	1,936	249	173	852
06-Apr-14	7,607	1,648	210	152	760
07-Apr-14	4,406	947	104	81	463

Figure 8.10b Horizontal Tabular Report

Date	01-Apr-14	02-Apr-14	03-Apr-14	04-Apr-14	05-Apr-14	06-Apr-14	07-Apr-14
All_d:All:Avg HT (Min)(Sum)	325	948	906	1,031	852	760	463
All_d:All:Abandoned Call (Vol)(Sum)	66	193	145	201	173	152	81
All_d:All:Call Offered (Vol)(Sum)	706	1,817	1,708	2,037	1,936	1,648	947
All_d:All:AHT Forecast Vs Actual (%)(Sum)	3,308	9,281	8,727	8,961	8,622	7,607	4,406
All_d:All:Blocking Rate (%)(Sum)	79	242	217	262	249	210	104
All_d:All:AHT Forecast Vs Actual (%)(Avg)	100	103	101	100	100	100	102
All_d:All:Abandoned Call (Vol)(Avg)	2	2	2	2	2	2	2
All_d:All:Avg HT (Min)(Avg)	10	11	11	11	10	10	11
All_d:All:Blocking Rate (%)(Avg)	2	3	3	3	3	3	2
All_d:All:Call Offered (Vol)(Avg)	21	20	20	23	23	22	22

SUMMARY

The ability of the capacity management process, to fulfil its core function of proactively eliminating capacity-caused service failure and risks, depend largely on the insight, robustness, timeliness, and quality of the reports produced by the process, and targeting the right audience. The success of the capacity management process largely depends on its visibility, and acceptability as a value adding process to the business; this can be driven through well articulated policy and procedure anchored capacity reporting.

Capacity reports should be targeted at senior management, business system owners, IT system owners, risk managers, external regulators, application and infrastructure support teams. Depending on the target audience, the reports should highlight some of the following:

- Current level of capacity utilization in business terms
- Current level of capacity utilization in technical terms
- Projected capacity utilization, both in business and technical terms
- Summary of major service incidents caused by capacity risk
- The status of ongoing capacity risks related projects
- The emerging capacity risks to be mitigated

ORGANIZATIONAL APPRAISAL

1. Do your capacity management process systems and procedures support the ability for users to acknowledge recent capacity breaches, new record business volumes and usage trends and where possible provide the justification?
2. Do you periodically produce formal capacity reports that suit the various stakeholders' need?
3. Does your capacity report comparatively show the previous, current, projected utilization and capacity limit of principal business metrics for the individual IT services in scope for capacity management?
4. Do your capacity management process systems and procedures, support self-service reporting for users?
5. Do your capacity management process systems and procedures support the users' ability to view a report using different chart options that is suitable for highlighting the issue at stake to the targeted audience?

9 CAPACITY PLANNING

"The person who says it cannot be done should not interrupt the person doing it"

– Chinese proverb

INTRODUCTION

Capacity planning is one of the key components of the capacity management process. The terms capacity planning, and capacity management are erroneously taken to mean the same thing, this is not right.

An organization's capacity management process is incomplete if the capacity planning aspect of the process is not undertaken. This is what is obtained in organizations where capacity management is taken to denote having different dashboards displaying infrastructure resource usage, and business volumetric.

Capacity Planning is about forecasting the computing and infrastructure resources that will be required to meet the business demand in the future. This is where the business, service, and resource metrics collected are translated into future business demand planning.

Capacity planning is driven by the business demand forecast information (data) provided by the business users or their representative about their anticipated increase/decrease in business activities or users.

Capacity planning involves the following main steps:

1. **Inputs:** Gathering information/data from the various capacity planning Inputs (discussed below, and shown in Table 9.1)

2. **Model:** Using the information/data from the inputs, build the capacity planning model; to forecast the resource requirement corresponding to the business demand forecast's input information/data.

3. **Output:** Using the capacity planning model, produce the **capacity plan** (the main output of the capacity management process).

CAPACITY PLANNING INPUTS

Table 9.1, lists and describes the various input required for capacity planning.

Table 9.1   Capacity Planning Inputs

Input Name	Input Description	Input Source

Business demand forecast data / information	• The business plan of the organization should be translated to measurable future business volumes for the IT service capacity planning it is being carried out for. Some examples of business demand forecast information/data are:
	
	  o The monthly daily trade volume is expected to increase by 30% in the next one year.
	
	  o For the next 6 months, fifty thousand new users will be
		Provided by the business user, using the identified principal business metric that drives capacity.

Table 9.1 (continued)

Input Name	Input Description	Input Source
	added to the system.	
Service Performance SLA	• Clear service performance SLA is critical input for capacity planning. Capacity planning is about making sure that the performance SLA is not breached.	Agreed between IT, business users, and the service manager
	• Ambiguous SLA should be avoided, for example, the SLA for a single sign-on system that states "Login response time must be less than 800 milliseconds" is ambiguous, because, it does not state under what business demand condition the SLA should hold. The SLA can be rephrased as "Login response time, must be less than 800 milliseconds for total user-accounts not greater than 5000". As a result, it is expected that the inputs- "Business demand forecast data" and "Service Performance SLA" are in sync.	
	• SLA is about provided service, hence, SLA should not be in technical term like "host server CPU utilization should	

133

Table 9.1 (continued)

Input Name	Input Description	Input Source
	not exceed 80%". This is not SLA, but resource usage information, and not measure of service delivery. Conversely, it is desirable to have applications that drive the host server CPU utilization as high as possible, as long as performance is not impacted.	
Historical business data	• The aggregated data of the principal business metric (that drives capacity).	From CDB
Historical Service Performance data	• The aggregated data of the service performance data – latency, throughput, concurrency etc.	From CDB
Historical Infrastructure resource usage data	• The aggregated data of the computing and infrastructure resource utilization data	From CDB
Performance Testing Result	• This report is required to provide the upper limits of the capacity planning model, as it affects the application's service performance (throughput, latency etc), and resource utilization.	Obtained from the application performance testing report

Table 9.1 (continued)

Input Name	Input Description	Input Source
The IT service scale up options	• There may not be need for capacity planning, if the target application cannot be scaled up. Consequently, there is need to know from the application's design, and architecture, what options are available for scaling either vertically or horizontally.	From application architecture documents
Assumptions	• Sometimes, assumptions are made when creating a capacity planning model for an application. These assumptions should be discussed with stakeholders, and included in the capacity plan report.	The assumptions are made by the capacity planner

CAPACITY PLANNING MODEL - FORECASTING SERVICE & RESOURCE

Capacity planning model is used to bring together the capacity planning inputs; to enable the forecasting of the infrastructure resource that will be required to cope with the predicted business demand, without service failure or performance degradation.

Capacity planning models are tailored to suit specific IT service. It may be difficult to have one model that is one-model-fits-all; as the application design, users behaviour, and service performance characteristics may vary. However, an existing capacity planning model may be with little tweaking, modified to suit another related IT service.

Figure 9.2, shows the flow diagram indicating the relationship between business demand, and infrastructure resource requirement.

Figure 9.2 Transition path: from business demand to infrastructure Requirement

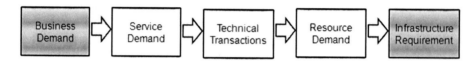

In the flow diagram, there are four stages in transition to predicting the infrastructure requirement, namely:

- **Stage#1: Business Demand** - this is a **known** variable, because it is provided by the user as one of the input for capacity planning. For example, new corporate clients are to be signed on in the next 12 months; as a result, the current daily trading volume is expected to increase by 10% every month (starting in 3 months time) over the next 12 months.

- **Stage#2: Service Demand** - this is an **unknown** variable, to be derived. The business demand needs to be translated to IT services. Examples of IT services are customer registration, account activation, order, statement download, etc. It is paramount that the services mix is derived using historical data.

- **Stage#3: Technical Transactions** - this is also an **unknown** variable, and needs to be derived. Each IT service can be made up of one or more technical transactions, for example, a single order can be made up of the following technical transactions: login, search item, add to basket, check out, etc. Also, the technical transactions mix should also be derived using historical data. For non-complex applications, sometimes, this stage is left out; however, models will generally provide better accuracy when this stage is included.

- **Stage#4: Resource Demand** - this is likewise an **unknown** variable, to be derived. The technical transactions drive the usage of the infrastructure and computing resources. The resource costs can include CPU, Storage space, memory, etc. It is expected that the unit cost of each technical transaction in terms of resources consumption, should be available from performance testing or analytical modelling.

- **Stage#5: Infrastructure Requirement forecast** - this is an **unknown** variable, to be derived using output from stage#4. The final infrastructure requirement will be dependent on the scale up options available for the service.

> **Success Hint:**
> *No growth in expected business demand does not automatically imply there is no need for capacity planning, performance can still be affected by other factors e.g. changing user demand pattern, growth in user activities, growth in historical data, etc.*

In simple term, capacity planning model seeks to predict the three unknown values. These unknowns can be found using any of the different prediction methods.

It may not be possible to create a capacity planning model that will forecast all the infrastructure resources. However, the focus should be on resources that are most likely to constitute a bottleneck (this can be obtained from the performance testing result, monitoring, or from previous capacity-caused incident root cause analysis reports). As a minimum, the following resource categories should be included in the modelling:

- **Concurrency:** system resources induced by concurrency requests; queuing up requests, and using up processing resources; and
- **Persistence:** System resources induced by persistence requests, which permanently use up storage space.

Capacity planning model, can be created using one or more of these prediction methods: estimates, trending, analytical models, simulation, or benchmarking; these are further discussed in Table 9.3.

CAPACITY PLANNING PREDICTION METHODS

The primary determinant of the prediction type to use is the balance between accuracy, and implementation cost. Table 9.3, compares the different prediction methods.

Table 9.3   Prediction Methods

Types	Description	Pros & Cons
Estimates	This prediction method is based on the user making some estimates based on experience, and knowledge of the application behaviour.	This is the fastest and cheapest prediction method. Unfortunately, it is a sure recipe for incurring service failure caused by inadequate capacity. This is an indication that the investment in

Table 9.3 (continued)

Types	Description	Pros & Cons
		the capacity management process is not yielding appropriate returns.
Trending	This prediction method uses the historical resource usage data; to forecast the future resource requirement through extrapolation.	This prediction method is very easy to apply, gives projected view, and has no dependencies. As a result, it can be applied directly on a single historical dataset to forecast the future.
	The key assumption in extrapolation is that "tomorrow will be same as today".	The trending functionality is commonly available in monitoring tools, and included in spreadsheets like Microsoft Excel.
	The figure shown directly below shows a typical forecasting based on linear trending, and the resultant erroneous trend line.	Conversely, this method is prone to inaccurate forecasting; as the key assumption used is erroneous. Capacity management process is about solving the problems associated with increasing business volume; hence the key assumption is wrong.

Danger of Linear Trending

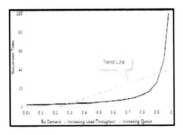

| | | Also, in response to linear load, the computer CPU response time and utilization behaves non-linearly due |

139

Table 9.3 (continued)

Types	Description	Pros & Cons
		to increasing queue as shown in figure on the left.
		This method does not take into cognizance the relationship between business demand, and resource usage. Therefore, it cannot be used for service performance forecasting or capacity planning.
		Prediction using trending method gives inconsistent result that is dependent on the starting point of the used historical dataset. In addition, its result is affected by stepwise change in the data.
Analytical Modelling	Analytical model prediction is based on using mathematical technique to represent activities of an IT system, and the changes in the system.	An analytic model is usually built with a limited, tailored and predefined workload mixes at a single point in time, hence, no single model is a one-model-fits-all.
	Analytical model is based on applying the queuing	Good for predicting computer CPU behaviour using the queuing

Table 9.3 (continued)

Types	Description	Pros & Cons
	theory to calculate the response times in a computer system.	network theory. However, the test required obtaining the "CPU cost per transaction", and "transaction response times" data required as input to the model; may be demanding.
	In computing, there is a new buzz word called "Machine Learning", the machine learning concept will potentially find use in the automated creation of analytical models. Machine learning is covered in subsequent chapter of this book.	Can be used for modelling system performance, and arrives at the same result as obtained from load testing, but without incurring the cost of the environment setup and the testing process. Generally, does not take much time to build, and has an accuracy level that is good enough for capacity planning.
Simulation Modelling	Simulation model predicts computer system performance by emulating both the dynamic and static structure, using discrete events.	This prediction method provides accurate forecast for both new application sizing, and modelling changes of an existing IT system if correctly setup. Requires good knowledge of the internal workings of a system, and takes more time to setup.

Table 9.3 (continued)

Types	Description	Pros & Cons
Benchmarking	Benchmarking applies real transactions to a physical hardware in order to measure the real application's processing performance. This is more suited for application sizing rather than for predicting performance and capacity planning.	Very good for determining the capacity limits and bottlenecks of system resources. Has good accuracy, nevertheless, requires the application running in its physical hardware.

CORRELATION - ESTABLISHING RELATIONSHIP BETWEEN DATASETS

In capacity modelling, there is a need to determine the existence of the predictive relationship between two or more variables. Where such relationship exists, then the dependent (unknown) variable can be predicted using the independent (known) variable. The process of determining the existence of predictive relationship between two or more variables is called correlation. Correlation is needed when building regression model, and may also be used in some aspects of the analytical model.

The correlation coefficient (R) is a measure of how good or strong the linear relationship is between two variables. R-squared (is also called R^2, or coefficient of determination) measures the level of correlation. Besides, it is a statistical measure of how close the data is to the fitted regression line. R-Squared (R^2) is the square of the correlation coefficient (R), hence it is called R-squared.

As previously stated in chapter 9, the closer R^2 value is to 1.0, the better the relationship, conversely, the closer the value is to zero (0), the worse the relationship. A value of 1.0 represents a perfect correlation. A positive R value means both variables are increasing in the same direction; while a negative value implies that as one variable increases, the other decreases. For capacity model to be reliable for capacity planning, R^2 value in the range of 0.80 to 1.0 should be targeted between the dependent and independent variables.

CORRELATION ANALYSIS USING MICROSOFT EXCEL

Excel has a function "correl(array1, array2)" that can be applied with a cell to calculate the correlation coefficient (R) value between dataset in two columns. However, if you have large number of datasets for which you want to find the R or R^2 values between the various data-pairs, you will need to use the Excel "Analysis ToolPak" add-ins.

Furthermore, the steps below outline a guide to calculating the R and R^2 values between multiple datasets using the Excel add-ins.

Step #1
Add the "Analysis ToolPak" add-in using the "Excel Options" as shown in Figure 9.4. Click on "Add-Ins" -> "Analysis ToolPak" ->"Go"

Figure 9.4   Excel Options

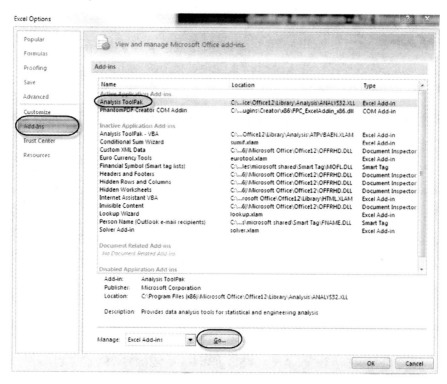

Step #2

Starting from "Data menu option", click on "Data Analysis" button, to open dialog box. From the box, select "Correlation", and click "OK".

Figure 9.5 Correlation Option

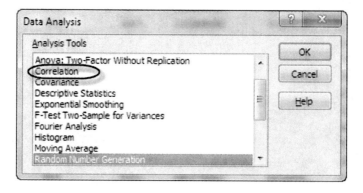

Step #3

Using the correlation input dialog box, shown in Figure 9.6, enter the details for the analysis.

Figure 9.6 Correlation Input Details

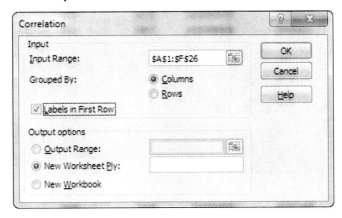

Ensure that:

- The Excel cells covered by the "Input Range" field value must contain only numeric data (except for the header column or row).
- your cell reference selection includes the column/row labels
- the "Labels in First Row/Column" is checked
- Figure 9.7, shows sample data used for the analysis, in specifying the input range, the **date column should be excluded**, otherwise, analysis will fail.

Figure 9.7 Sample input data for correlation analysis

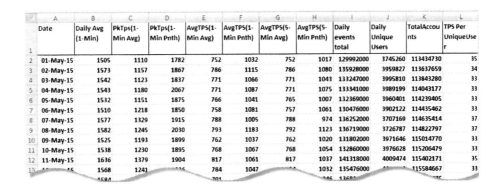

Date	Daily Avg (1-Min)	PkTps(1-Min Avg)	PkTps(1-Min Pnth)	AvgTPS(1-Min Avg)	AvgTPS(1-Min Pnth)	AvgTPS(5-Min Avg)	AvgTPS(5-Min Pnth)	Daily events total	Daily Unique Users	TotalAccounts	TPS Per UniqueUser
01-May-15	1505	1110	1782	752	1032	752	1017	129992000	3745260	113434730	35
02-May-15	1573	1157	1867	786	1115	786	1080	135928000	3959827	113637659	34
03-May-15	1542	1123	1837	771	1066	771	1043	133247000	3995810	113843280	33
04-May-15	1543	1180	2067	771	1087	771	1075	133341000	3989199	114043177	33
05-May-15	1532	1151	1875	766	1041	765	1007	132369000	3960401	114239405	33
06-May-15	1510	1218	1850	758	1081	757	1061	130476000	3902122	114435462	33
07-May-15	1577	1329	1915	788	1005	788	974	136252000	3707169	114635414	37
08-May-15	1582	1245	2030	793	1183	792	1123	136719000	3726787	114822797	37
09-May-15	1525	1193	1899	762	1037	762	1020	131802000	3971646	115014770	33
10-May-15	1538	1230	1895	768	1067	768	1054	132860000	3976628	115206479	33
11-May-15	1636	1379	1904	817	1061	817	1037	141318000	4009474	115402171	35
15	1568	1241		784	1047		1032	135476000		115584667	33
	1584			701			246	12602			

Then, click on the "OK" button, to have Excel generate the correlation coefficient (R) value comparative table in a new worksheet. Sample output is shown in Figure 9.8.

Figure 9.8 Sample output correlation analysis showing R values

R	Daily Avg (1-Min)	PkTps(1-Min Avg)	PkTps(1-Min Pnth)	AvgTPS(1-Min Avg)	AvgTPS(1-Min Pnth)	AvgTPS(5-Min Avg)	AvgTPS(5-Min Pnth)	Daily events total	Daily Unique Users	TotalAccounts	TPS Per UniqueUser
Daily Avg (1-Min)	1.00										
PkTps(1-Min Avg)	0.58	1.00									
PkTps(1-Min Pnth)	0.31	0.74	1.00								
AvgTPS(1-Min Avg)	0.41	0.90	0.63	1.00							
AvgTPS(1-Min Pnth)	0.34	0.85	0.79	0.89	1.00						
AvgTPS(5-Min Avg)	0.41	0.90	0.63	1.00	0.89	1.00					
AvgTPS(5-Min Pnth)	0.33	0.85	0.77	0.90	0.99	0.90	1.00				
Daily events total	1.00	0.58	0.31	0.41	0.34	0.41	0.33	1.00			
Daily Unique Users	- 0.02	0.21	0.11	0.29	0.24	0.29	0.26	- 0.02	1.00		
TotalAccounts	- 0.68	- 0.60	- 0.55	- 0.33	- 0.40	- 0.33	- 0.37	- 0.68	- 0.04	1.00	
TPS Per UniqueUser	1.00	0.56	0.30	0.38	0.32	0.38	0.30	1.00	- 0.10	- 0.67	1.00

The value on each cell shows the correlation coefficient or R value, between the metrics specified on the row and column header respectively. Values closer to 1.0 indicates that an increase in row-level metric, also causes the column-level metric to increase; while those closer to -1.0 is the reverse.

Step #4

The R^2 can also be computed by mirroring the R value table and multiplying each R value by itself. The R^2 is the actual determinant of how well the metric-pair is related, hence, it is the basis for making the decision to use, or not to use the metric-pair in capacity planning model. The R^2 derived from R table is shown in Figure 9.9, the cells are formatted to highlight R^2 values; where good or acceptable relationship exists.

Figure 9.9 R² values computed from the R value table

R^2	Daily Avg (1-Min)	PkTps(1-Min Avg)	PkTps(1-Min Pnth)	AvgTPS(1-Min Avg)	AvgTPS(1-Min Pnth)	AvgTPS(5-Min Avg)	AvgTPS(5-Min Pnth)	Daily events total	Daily Unique Users	TotalAccounts	TPS Per UniqueUser
Daily Avg (1-Min)	1.00										
PkTps(1-Min Avg)	0.34	1.00									
PkTps(1-Min Pnth)	0.10	0.54	1.00								
AvgTPS(1-Min Avg)	0.17	0.81	0.40	1.00							
AvgTPS(1-Min Pnth)	0.12	0.72	0.63	0.78	1.00						
AvgTPS(5-Min Avg)	0.17	0.81	0.40	1.00	0.78	1.00					
AvgTPS(5-Min Pnth)	0.11	0.73	0.59	0.81	0.99	0.81	1.00				
Daily events total	1.00	0.34	0.10	0.17	0.12	0.17	0.11	1.00			
Daily Unique Users	0.00	0.04	0.01	0.08	0.06	0.08	0.07	0.00	1.00		
TotalAccounts	0.46	0.36	0.30	0.11	0.16	0.11	0.14	0.46	0.00	1.00	
TPS Per UniqueUser	0.99	0.31	0.09	0.14	0.10	0.14	0.09	0.99	0.01	0.45	1.00

For example, from Figure 9.9, it can be seen that the following metric-pairs have acceptable R² values:

- Daily events total vs. Daily Avg TPS (1-Min),
- TPS Per UniqueUser vs. Daily events total, and
- TPS Per UniqueUser vs. Daily Avg TPS (1-Min) are related to each other, hence, can be derived from the other, and vice versa.

Success Hint:

Correlation Coefficient (R) and R-square (R²) values are bound to change as customers/users activity pattern changes; hence, the correlation analysis should be refreshed each time it is to be used in a capacity model, with the most recent daily/weekly/monthly data.

SUMMARY

Capacity planning is one of the key components of the capacity management process, and drives the process' ability to proactively manage capacity. The capacity management process is incomplete, and may not be able to fulfil the process' goal if the capacity planning component is overlooked. The output from the capacity planning activity is the "capacity plan"

Capacity Planning is about forecasting the computing and infrastructure resources that will be required to meet the business demand in future. This is where the business, service, and resource metrics collected are translated, using a model to forecast future infrastructure requirements.

Capacity planning models can be simple or complex, but the accuracy is what matters most. The capacity model can use any of the prediction methods; however, it should be remembered that linear trending is based on the assumption that "tomorrow will be like today" which is not true in business, and secondly, system resources (especially CPU) do not behave linearly.

ORGANIZATIONAL APPRAISAL

1. As part of the capacity management process, is capacity planning activity carried out for your IT services?
2. For your IT services, is capacity planning carried out using model driven by business metrics?
3. Do the business users get involved in the capacity planning by providing the demand forecast data, and participating in reviewing the model?
4. Do you have service level agreement with the business users that drives your capacity planning performance target?
5. How reliable are the prediction methods that your capacity planning models are based on.

10 BUILDING ANALYTICAL CAPACITY PLANNING MODEL

"A goal without a plan is just a wish"
- Antoine de Saint-Exupery.

INTRODUCTION

Capacity planning model is the representation of real world IT system's performance using a mathematical framework, with a view to predicting the computing resources needed to operate within specified target performance level for a given business demand volume.

The step by step process for building a capacity planning model for a geographical imaging application/system will be described here. This sample capacity planning model to be described here is based on the application component providing the worst performance bottleneck – the storage system. For the purpose of this write up, the storage system we will describe in this capacity modelling exercise is called A2Z C-480 Storage system (the same model can be applied for other storage types like IBM, EMC, just by little tweaking and changing the type-specific limits/maximum capacity limits in the model configuration).

I have chosen to use a storage system, to practically demonstrate how to create a typical capacity planning model because the storage system is generic and can be understood by most readers of this book.

A storage system is a high-capacity and expandable networked storage system that is made up of arrays of SAN disks, powerful multi-core processors, 64-bit operating system, fibre channel, with its own internal application that controls and manages its data storage and retrieval operations. Examples of storage systems are: CLARiion EMC® CX4 960, CLARiion EMC FC4700, IBM® DS8870, etc.

For any application that uses an external storage system like those specified above, sometimes the application's major performance bottleneck could be its storage system component. Therefore, it is important that this critical and often shared infrastructure component of an IT system has its own capacity planning model.

MODELLING OBJECTIVE

IT application to be identified as "Geomap" is used for storing satellite images of cities across the globe, and retrieval of the stored images as requested by users over the internet.

For this application, the most likely component that will introduce performance issue for users of the dependent application is the storage system known as "A2Z C-480".

The modelling objective of the "A2Z C-480" storage system is to predict, based on the provided business demand forecast, the following:

1. When additional disk drives should be added.
2. When the current storage system unit reaches its capacity limit (when more disk drives cannot be added); add another unit of the "A2Z C-480" storage system.

Based on the model prediction, doing the above will ensure that the storage system component does not constitute a performance risk.

"A2Z" STORAGE SYSTEM MODEL - PERFORMANCE RESTRAINT RESOURCES

Based on the information provided in Figure 10.1, performance degradation and capacity issue will set in under any of these conditions:

1. **Storage Space Resource**: the storage space resource demand exceeds the total available space that the existing storage system unit(s) can offer (that is, when all disk drive slots of the existing storage system unit(s) are used up).
2. **File Count Limit Resource**: the storage system firmware can only support about 16 billion files. It means that no more image files can be saved after this limit is reached, until an additional storage unit is added.
3. **Input-Output (IO) Resource:** the recommended maximum I/O per second (IOPS) per disk for optimal performance is shown in Figure 10.1. The implications are:
    a. Each request for image file requires the I/O resource
    b. To ensure performance is not degraded, the total IOPS from users should not exceed the total IOPS available from all disks in the storage system unit(s). If exceeded, additional disk drives will be required to further distribute the I/O requests, and keep performance within SLA.
    c. When disk drives can no longer be added to augment for I/O resource demand, then an additional storage unit will be required.

From the above, it can be concluded that:
*   The need for additional disk drives can be triggered by storage space resource, or I/O resource demand.

- The need to additional storage system units can be triggered by any of these: storage space, or IOPS resources, or by the File count limitation.

Figure 10.1 Storage System Architecture & Technical Limitations

A2Z C-480 Storage System Architecture & Technical Limitations	
Architecture Information	
In the A2Z C-480 there are 6 Disk Array Enclosures (DAEs) of 300GB FC drives and 6 DAEs of 1TB SATA drives	
One of the FC DAEs is used for system and hotspares	
The FC disks are to be used for Production (Live)	
FC Disk will be made up of the 300GB and 450GB Disks	
Additional A2Z C-480 may be installed in the future	

Configuration Parameter	Value
Number of A2Z AZ-480 System units	1
Actual Allocated FC & SATA Drives	75
Actual Allocated FC-300GB Drives	75
Actual Allocated FC-450GB Drives	
Actual Allocated SATA-1TB Drives	
Number of Disks Allocation (System & Hot Spares)	21
Number of Disks Allocation	84
Max DAE Per System	32
Max Drives per DAE	15
Max Drives per system	480
FC-300GB Drives Allocation Available for Data (RAID)	60
FC-450GB Drives Allocation Available for Data (RAID)	
SATA-1TB Drives Allocation Available for Data (RAID)	
Recommended IOPS for best performance	
IOPS per disk -FC-300GB-15K-RPM	200
IOPS per disk -FC-450GB-15K-RPM	180
IOPS per disk -SATA-1TB-7.2K-RPM	90
A2Z Files Limit	
A2Z Firmware File Limit per file system (million)	16384 (16TB)

Success Hint:

The knowledge of application architecture and inherent limitations are good input for building reliable capacity planning model.

MODELLING APPROACH

The model will treat the "A2Z C-480" storage system as an application, and its capacity planning will be based on using the ITIL capacity management process framework's three sub processes: business, service, and resource. By applying the business demand, the model will forecast the additional disks, and A2Z system units that will be required at anytime.

The Figure 10.2 shows the resource forecasting flow diagram: "Business Demand" -> "Service Demand Forecast" -> "Resource Demand Forecast" -> "Infrastructure Forecast of additional disks (or A2Z System units)".

Figure 10.2 Modelling Forecasting flow diagrams

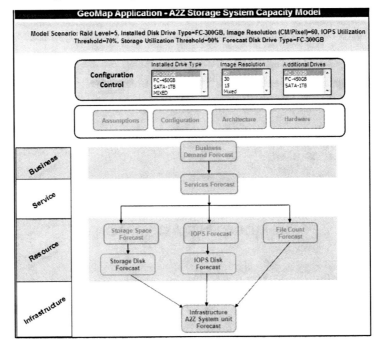

The model is developed using Microsoft Excel. The model summary view and data flow is shown in Figure 10.2. The main components are:

1. **Model scenario**: this describes the model based on the selection from the configuration control.

2. **Configuration control**: this serves as the "Technical What-if" panel, for users to understand how changing the options impacts the ultimate infrastructure forecast.

3. **Model information navigation buttons**: each button is used to access the information used in the model. The architecture and configuration information are shown in Figure 10.1, while assumptions and hardware will be discussed later.

4. **Business**: this is the business demand layer of the model, where the expected demand from the business is entered in the model. It also provides the input for the "Business-What-if" checks.

5. **Service**: this is the service demand layer, and how the business demand gets mapped to technical services.

6. **Resource**: in this component, the technical services are used as input to predict the infrastructure and computing resources utilization.

7. **Infrastructure**: the result from resource utilization forecast is then used to predict the physical infrastructure e.g. disk drives, storage system units to be installed, and the time they should be in place to avoid service degradation or failure.

THE MODELLING ASSUMPTIONS

Very often, capacity models will usually be based on some assumptions. It is standard practice to ensure that these assumptions are clearly communicated to users in the capacity plan derived from the model. Figure 10.3 shows the assumptions used for A2Z storage system modelling.

Figure 10.3 Modelling Assumptions

S/N	Description
1	Forecast is based on requirement to meet Storage, IOPS Performance and Number of Files
2	Only A2Z C-480 backend is considered, the swtich and NAS components not considered
3	RAID 5 Level used
4	File Access Type = Random
5	Backup Requirement out of scope as this depends on backup strategy and policy
6	Predominant IO Size for map tiles request is <= 16KB
7	Number IO Per Image Request is independent of the Image Resolution used
8	Lost users not accounted for
9	Cache not considered as more cache mean better IOPS (higer IOPS)

INFORMATION FROM HISTORICAL METRICS

The monitoring, data collection, aggregation, and storage activities of the capacity management process find their ultimate use in capacity planning. From the historical metrics, the basic operational characteristics, service consumption pattern, and computing resource usage can be established; and serves as an input to the capacity model. Figure 10.4, shows the information obtained from the historical metrics.

Figure 10.4 Modelling input from historical capacity metrics

A2Z C-480 Storage System: Production Environment Operational characteristics from Historical metrics											
Description	Jan 17	Feb 17	Mar 17	Apr 17	May 17	Jun 17	Jul 17	Aug 17	Sep 17	Oct 17	Nov
MEASURED - Number Host IO Per Image Request	5	5	5	5	5	5	5	5	5	5	
MEASURED - Percenatge of Daily Users at Peak Hour (%)	25%	25%	25%	25%	25%	25%	25%	25%	25%	25%	25
MEASURED - Requests Peak-to-Average Ratio @ Peak	1.25	1.25	1.25	1.25	1.25	1.25	1.25	1.25	1.25	1.25	
MEASURED - IO Read Proportion (%)	90%	90%	90%	90%	90%	90%	90%	90%	90%	90%	90
MEASURED - IO Write Proportion (%)	10%	10%	10%	10%	10%	10%	10%	10%	10%	10%	

Specific to Figure 10.4, note the followings:

- Items shown for "Jan'17" to "Apr'17" in darker grey colour are aggregated actual measurements of the production environment from data held in the capacity database (CDB), hence these are prefixed as "MEASURED".

155

- The same "MEASURED" value will be applied for subsequent forecast, starting from "May'17".

- Single image request resource cost is known – "Number of Host I/O per Image Request", and can be changed in the model if the need arises.

- The measurement "Percentage of Daily User at peak Hour (%)" is significant for determining the peak request in a day. For example, if this value is 10%, and in a day, the total number of users requesting map tiles images is 360000. It implies that at the peak hour, 360000 x (10 / 100), i.e. 36000 users were active. Using the hourly average 360000 / 24 i.e. 15000 active users will lead to unreliable capacity planning.

- The measurement "Requests Peak-to-Average Ratio @ Peak Hour" is also important, as it helps to estimate the peak within the peak hour. For example, if this value is 1.2, and at the peak hour, the request count is 36000. It indicates average request per second is 36000 / (60*60) .i.e. 10. Applying the peak-to-average ratio of 1.2, the peak request per second to be used in the model will be 12 (1.2 x 10).

The principles stated for the storage system can also be applied for modelling applications requests to a server infrastructure by replacing the storage metrics and parameters with equivalents. For example:

- The storage I/O Cost ("Number of Host I/O per Image Request") can be replaced by equivalent CPU cost or service time of the composite technical services.

- The I/O Read/Write Proportion (%) can be replaced with the proportions from the various technical transaction mixes of a service request. For example, an online flight booking request can consist of the following technical transactions:
    o 30% Login page
    o 40% Flight Picker page

- o 3% New user registration page
- o 5% Flight Amendment page
- o 2% Profile update page
- o 10% Payment page
- o 10% Online Check-in page

BUSINESS DEMAND FORECAST

The requirement to Increase the infrastructure capacity should be driven and justified by the business demand forecast. "Business Demand Forecast" as is often called, is the business planning information that can impact volume of business activities in the near future. This information should be provided by the business, to the capacity planning team. In addition, other good practices regarding business demand forecast are:

- The business demand forecast data should also be stored in the capacity database
- During a model refresh, the prior demand "Forecast" provided by the business should be compared with the measured demand "Actual" of the same period; so as to test the reliability of the previously provided forecast data. It is good practice that forecast/actual variations in excess of +/- 10%, should trigger the business reviewing their forecast figures.
- Most importantly, a capacity planning model's accuracy is directly dependent on the correctness of the business demand forecast figures.
- In the capacity planning model, the business demand forecast should drive the "What-if" scenarios. Consequently, changing the business demand forecast numbers should reflect in the predicted resources' utilization.

157

Figure 10.5 Business Demand Forecast – Tabular Data View

Business Demand Forecast										
Description	Jan'17	Feb'17	Mar'17	Apr'17	May'17	Jun'17	J...	Dec'17	Jan'18	Feb'18	Mar'18
FORECAST - New Cities (#)	2500	400	300	300	250	200	40	40	40	70	75
FORECAST - Cummulative Cities (#)	2500	2900	3200	3500	3750	3950	...0	4490	4530	4600	4675
FORECAST - Daily User Map Tiles Request (Million)	775	853	938	1032	1135	1248	...11	2212	2433	2676	2944

Figures 10.5 and 10.6 exhibit the business demand forecast used for the A2Z storage system modelling. As shown in Figure 10.5, the load to this storage system that will impact the capacity is expected to come from two primary sources; changing any of them will affect the resulting resource and physical infrastructure forecast.

Based on the design of the application "GeoMap" using this "A2Z Storage system", the two principal business capacity drivers, and their associated capacity-request types are shown in Table 10.6.

Table 10.7 Business Demand Capacity Driver Analysis

Business Demand	Request Type	Resource Affected	Resource Shortage Implication
New Cities	Persistence (permanent storage space usage -arising from newly acquired map tile files, from the new cities to be added)	Storage Space limit per A2Z unit. File count limit per A2Z unit.	If the available total storage of A2Z is used up, subsequent acquired city map tiles cannot be stored, except a new A2Z unit is added. Also if the number of acquired city map tiles files reaches the 16 billion A2Z firmware limit, new files cannot be added.

Table 10.7   (continued)

Business Demand	Request Type	Resource Affected	Resource Shortage Implication
Daily Users Map Tiles Request	Concurrency (arising from users requesting for map tiles at the same time)	Input-Output Operations per second (IOPS) limit per A2Z unit.	When the I/O requests to the storage system exceed the available capacity (determined by number of disk drives, and types), the surplus I/O requests will be in a queue, and served when I/O resources are freed up. Unlike persistence request type that reaches hard capacity limit, concurrency request type only reaches soft capacity limit. The implication of soft capacity limit is that additional requests add to the I/O request queue length, meaning that users requesting map tiles will begin to experience degraded performance (increased time to fetch image). Over time as the queue increases, the service may eventually fail – users will not be able to access the image files.

Note that as new cities map tiles are acquired, the total (cumulative) cities with map tiles in the application increases, consequently, the daily request for map tiles increases. The Figure 10.6 depicts this demand behaviour.

Figure 10.6 Business Demand Forecast – Graphical Data View

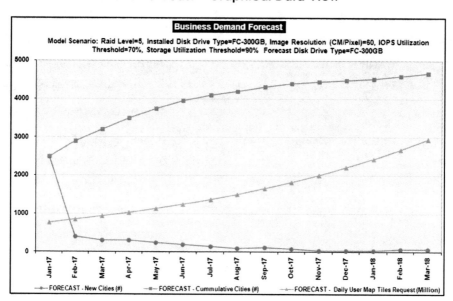

SERVICE DEMAND FORECAST

The objective of service demand forecast is to translate the business demand forecast to the corresponding business services of the application, and finally derive the equivalent technical services. The actual consumer of the infrastructure and computing resources is the technical service request.

For the "A2Z Storage System" under review, the two main technical services are namely:

- Concurrency Request – Disk IOPS

- Persistence Request – Storage Space

Note that the "Number of Image files" is not a technical service but a limitation that can result in capacity risk, and its growth forecast will be considered in the model.

Figure 10.7, shows the technical services forecast, derived from the business demand forecast data input, and the option selected by the user from the "Configuration and Scenario Information" of Figure 10.8.

Figure 10.7 Service Request Forecast

Service Requests (Forecast)											
Concurrency Request - Disk IOPS											
Description	Jan'17	Feb'17	Mar'17	Apr'17	May'17	Jun'17	Jul'17	17	Dec'17	Jan'18	Feb'18
FORECAST - Peak User MapTiles Requests per second	2804	3084	3393	3732	4105	4516	496 272		8000	8800	9680
Persistence Request - Storage Space											
Description	Jan'17	Feb'17	Mar'17	Apr'17	May'17	Jun'17	Jul'17		Dec'17	Jan'18	Feb'18
Storage/City (GB)@60 CM/Pixel Resolution	3.50	3.50	3.50	3.50	3.50	3.50	3.50		3.50	3.50	3.50
Storage/City (GB)@30 CM/Pixel Resolution	0.00	0.00	0.00	0.00	0.00	0.00	0.00	00	0.00	0.00	0.00
Storage/City (GB)@15 CM/Pixel Resolution	0.00	0.00	0.00	0.00	0.00	0.00	0.00	00	0.00	0.00	0.00
Storage (GB)/City	3.50	3.50	3.50	3.50	3.50	3.50	3.50	50	3.50	3.50	3.50
FORECAST - Monthly CitySphere Storage (TB)	8.54	1.37	1.03	1.03	0.85	0.68	0.51	4	0.14	0.14	0.24
FORECAST - Monthly LandSphere Storage (TB)	5.00	0.00	0.00	0.00	0.00	0.00	0.00		0.00	0.00	0.00
FORECAST - Total Monthly Storage (TB)	13.54	1.37	1.03	1.03	0.85	0.68	0.51		0.14	0.14	0.24
Persistence Request - No of Image-Files											
Description	Jan'17	Feb'17	Mar'17	Apr'17	May'17	Jun'17	Jul'17	17	Dec'17	Jan'18	Feb'18
File Count/City (GB)@60 CM/Pixel Resolution	50000	50000	50000	50000	50000	50000	50000 000		50000	50000	50000
File Count/City (GB)@30 CM/Pixel Resolution	0	0	0	0	0	0	0	0	0	0	0
File Count/City (GB)@15 CM/Pixel Resolution	0	0	0	0	0	0	0		0	0	0
File Count/City	50000	50000	50000	50000	50000	50000	50000		50000	50000	50000
FORECAST - Monthly CitySphere Files Count (Million)	125	20	15	15	13	10	8 2		2	2	4
FORECAST - Monthly LandSphere Files Count (Million)	54	0	0	0	0	0	0		0	0	0
FORECAST - Total Monthly Files Count (Million)	179	20	15	15	13	10	8 2		2	2	4

In Figure 10.7, the image quality is determined by the selected pixel resolution option. The selected resolution also determines the amount of storage space to be consumed.

Note that the "FORECAST - Peak User Map Tiles Requests **per second**", was derived using the "FORECAST - **Daily** User Map Tiles Request (Million)" demand forecast, the peak factors, and the "Peak Requests per day" translated to "Peak Requests per second", thus:

"FORECAST - Peak User Map Tiles Requests per second" =

("FORECAST Daily User Map Tiles Request (Million)" x 1000000 x "MEASURED Percentage of Daily Users at Peak Hour (%)" x "MEASURED - Requests Peak-to-Average Ratio @ Peak Hour") / (24 x 60 x 60)

Figure 10.8 Configuration & Scenario Information

Application Configuration & Scenario Information		
SatelliteImages Resolution (CM/Pixel)	Estimated No of Image Files per City	Estimated Storage Space (GB) per City
60	50,000	3.5
30	210,000	7.5
15	850,000	10.5
Disk Drive Interface	Formatted Disk Capacity (GB)	Disks/ RAID Group	PARITY Disk/ RAID Group
FC-300GB	272.00	5	1
FC-450GB	372.50	5	1
SATA-1TB	931.50	5	1

RESOURCE UTILIZATION FORECAST

Using technical service forecast numbers, the next activity for capacity modelling is deriving the resource utilization or usage forecast. The computed forecasts for IOPS, Storage Spaces, and File count are shown in Figures 10.9, 10.10, and 10.11 respectively.

1. IO Resource Forecast

Figure 10.9, shows how the IOPS forecast is derived. The number of IOPS available in a drive is based on the drive type. Thus the model is designed to allow for "what-if" options for different disk drive types.

Figure 10.9 IOPS Resource Forecast

Input Output Per Second (IOPS) Forecast

Description	Jan'17	Feb'17	Mar'17	Apr'17	May'17	Jun'17	...	Nov'17	Dec'17	Jan'18	Feb'18	Mar'18
FORECAST - Peak Host IOPS	14019	15421	16963	18659	20525	22578	2?	36362	39998	43998	48398	53238
FORECAST - Peak Disk IOPS (Load)	18225	20048	22052	24258	26683	29352	74	47271	51998	57198	62918	69209
INSTALLED - IOPS -FC-300GB Drives	15000	15000	15000	15000	15000	15000	1?	15000	15000	15000	15000	15000
INSTALLED - IOPS -FC-450GB Drives	0	0	0	0	0	0	0	0	0	0	0	0
INSTALLED - IOPS -SATA-1TB Drives	0	0	0	0	0	0	0	0	0	0	0	0
INSTALLED - Total IOPS (All Drives)	15000	15000	15000	15000	15000	15000	1?	15000	15000	15000	15000	15000
ACTUAL - Peak Host IOPS Measured	18001	20070	21990	24305	0	0	0	0	0	0	0	

From the Figure 10.9, of IOPS resource forecast, to meet performance requirement from IOPS resource perspective, more disk drives will be required when the "INSTALLED Total IOPS (All Dives)" IOPS is less than "FORECAST Peak Disk IOPS (Load)". Note, adding more disk drives will be a capacity expansion; the option is good only if the A2Z Storage system unit has space to accommodate more drives.

2. Storage Space Resource Forecast

Storage space forecast is dependent on the disk drive type, and the RAID type.

Figure 10.10 Storage Space Forecast

Storage Space Forecast

Description	Jan'17	Feb'17	Mar'17	Apr'17	May'17	Jun'17	...	Nov'17	Dec'17	Jan'18	Feb'18	Mar'18
INSTALLED - Allocated FC-300GB Storage for data RAID5 (GB)	16320	16320	16320	16320	16320	16320	1? 16320	16320	16320	16320	16320	16320
INSTALLED - Allocated FC-450GB Storage for data RAID5 (GB)	0	0	0	0	0	0	0	0	0	0	0	0
INSTALLED - Allocated SATA-1TB Storage for data RAID5 (GB)	0	0	0	0	0	0	0	0	0	0	0	0
INSTALLED - Allocated (FC & SATA) Storage for data RAID5 (TB)	15.94	15.94	15.94	15.94	15.94	15.94	15.94	15.94	15.94	15.94	15.94	15.94
ACTUAL - Allocated Storage for data (TB) @ 90% Threshold RAID5	14.34	14.34	14.34	14.34	14.34	14.34	14.34	14.34	14.34	14.34	14.34	14.34
FORECAST - Total Storage Allocation (TB)	13.54	14.91	15.94	16.96	17.82	18.50	20.21	20.35	20.48	20.72	20.98	
ACTUAL - Total Measured Storage Usage (TB)	13.48	14.92	15.85	16.70								

From the Figure 10.10 of storage space resource forecast, to meet storage space requirement, more disk drives will be required when the "INSTALLED Allocated (FC & SATA) Storage for data RAID5 (TB)" is less than "FORECAST Total Storage Allocation (TB)". Note, adding more disk drives will be a capacity expansion option; and good only if the A2Z Storage system unit has space to accommodate more drives.

3. File count Resource Forecast

When the "FORECAST Cumulative Files Count (Millions)" exceeds the "INSTALLED Storage System File Count Limit (Mil)", the unit will not be able to accept new image files. Consequently, a new A2Z system unit will be required.

Figure 10.11 Image Files Count Forecast

Image File Count Forecast											
Description	Jan'17	Feb'17	Mar'17	Apr'17	May'17	Jun'17	Nov'17	Dec'17	Jan'18	Feb'18	Mar'18
INSTALLED - Storage System File Count Limit (Mil)	16384	16384	16384	16384	16384	16384	16384	16384	16384	16384	16384
FORECAST - Cummulative Files Count (Millions)	179	199	214	229	242	252	277	279	281	284	288
FORECAST - A2Z System unit (#)	1	1	1	1	1	1	1	1	1	1	1
ACTUAL - Cummulative Files Count (Million)	178	201	215	228							

The reliability and accuracy of the computed resource forecast can be checked using the "ACTUAL" for the previous months, as obtained from the monitoring tool or the capacity database.

> **Success Hint:**
>
> *Models should regularly be refreshed with actual data. The Actual vs. Forecast data should be reviewed as it provides the basis to check the accuracy level of the model, and continual fit-for-purpose.*

INFRASTRUCTURE FORECAST

The ultimate aim of the capacity planning model is to accurately forecast the physical infrastructure that will be required to adequately support the business demand for now and in future without performance degradation or service failure.

From our capacity planning model, the GeoMap application using the "A2Z Storage System" will require either:

- Additional disk drives to be installed in the existing A2Z Storage system unit(s), to boost IOPS or storage space resource needs, or
- Distribute the resource demand by adding new A2Z storage system unit(s) to the existing units.

1a. Additional disk forecast driven by storage Space resource

The forecast of the additional disk drives (based on storage space resource demand) that will be required each month is presented in Figure 10.12a, by the "FORECAST Additional Disk @FC-300GB RAID5 (#)".

Figure 10.12a Additional Disk Drive Count Forecast (from storage space resource)

Storage Space - Additional Disk Forecast											
Description	Jan'17	Feb'17	Mar'17	Apr'17	May'17	Jun'17	Nov'17	Dec'17	Jan'18	Feb'18	Mar'18
INSTALLED - Allocated Storage for data (TB) @ 90% Threshold RAID5	14.34	14.34	14.34	14.34	14.34	14.34	14.34	14.34	14.34	14.34	14.34
FORECAST - Total Storage Allocation (TB)	13.54	14.91	15.94	16.96	17.82	18.50	20.21	20.35	20.48	20.72	20.98
FORECAST - Total Storage Allocation Shortfall (GB)	0	582	1632	2682	3557	4257	6007	6147	6287	6532	6795
FORECAST - Additional Disk @FC-300GB RAID5 (#)	0	5	10	15	20	20	30	30	30	35	35
FORECAST - Additional Disk @FC-450GB RAID5 (#)	0	5	10	10	15	15	25	25	25	25	25
FORECAST - Additional Disk @SATA-1TB RAID5 (#)	0	5	5	5	5	10	10	10	10	10	10
FORECAST - Additional Disk @FC-300GB RAID5 (#)	0	5	10	15	20	20	30	30	30	35	35

The graphical view is shown in Fig 10.12b, for the different disk drives types. More disk drives will be required when the FC-300GB drives are used, and less when the SATA-1TB drives are used.

Figure 10.12b Additional Disk Drive Count Forecast (from storage space resource)

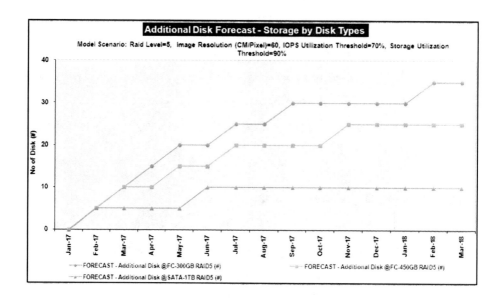

1b. Additional disk forecast driven by I/O resource

The forecast of the additional disk drives (based on IOPS resource demand) that will be required each month is displayed in Figure 10.13a, by the "FORECAST Additional Disk @FC-300GB-15K-RPM (#)".

Figure 10.13a Additional Disk Drive Count Forecast (from I/O resource)

Input Output Per Second (IOPS) - Additional Disk Forecast											
Description	Jan'17	Feb'17	Mar'17	Apr'17	May'17	Jun'17	Nov'17	Dec'17	Jan'18	Feb'18	Mar'18
INSTALLED - Total IOPS @70% Threshold - RAID5	10500	10500	10500	10500	10500	10500	10500	10500	10500	10500	10500
FORECAST - Peak Disk IOPS (Load)	18225	20048	22052	24258	26683	29352	47271	51998	57198	62918	69209
FORECAST - Total IOPS Shortfall	7725	9548	11552	13758	16183	18852	36771	41498	46698	52418	58709
FORECAST - Additional Disk - FC-300GB-15K-RPM	40	50	60	70	85	95	185	210	235	265	295
FORECAST - Additional Disk - FC-450GB-15K-RPM	45	55	65	80	90	105	205	235	260	295	330
FORECAST - Additional Disk - SATA-1TB-7.2K-RPM	90	110	130	155	180	210	410	465	520	585	655
FORECAST - Additional Disk - FC-300GB-15K-RPM	40	50	60	70	85	95	185	210	235	265	295

Figure 10.13b Additional Disk Drive Count Forecast (from I/O resource)

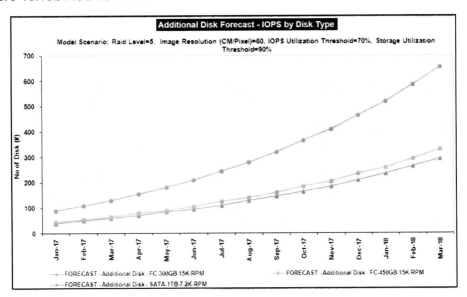

2. Additional A2Z Storage System Units Forecast

When the A2Z storage system unit has reached its disk drive expansion limit, such that new disk drives cannot be added, then it is time to add a new unit of the storage system. The implication is that the load traffic can split between the storage system units, thus ensuring the dependent application's SLA is not breached.

Figure 10.14, shows the made-up manufacturer's performance guideline for the A2Z storage system; in application capacity modelling, this can be likened to application latency and performance target specified in the SLA. Raising the threshold of any of the performance options, will delay the time for upgrading the infrastructure capacity, but will result in performance degradation.

Figure 10.14 A2Z Manufacture's Performance Guide – for Model Tuning

Hardware Performance Information	
A2Z C-480 Drives Usage Threshold	80%
IOPS Utilization Usage Threshold	70%
Storage Utilization Usage Threshold	90%
A2Z C-480 Drive Count Threshold for Best IOPS Performance	70%
A2Z Firmware File Limit per file system (million)	16384

Figure 10.15a forecast of A2Z storage system unit(s)

A2Z C-480 Storage System Units - Forecast by Storage, IOPS, and File Count												
Service Component	Description	Jan'17	Feb'17	Mar'17	Apr'17	May'17	Oct'17	Nov'17	Dec'17	Jan'18	Feb'18	Mar'18
Storage & IOPS	Storage: FORECAST - Additional Disk @FC-300GB RAID5 (#)	0	5	10	15	20	30	30	30	30	35	35
	IOPS: FORECAST - Additional Disk - FC-300GB-15K-RPM Used	40	50	60	70	85	165	185	210	235	265	295
	FORECAST - Additional Disk (FC-300GB) Drives #	40	50	60	70	85	165	185	210	235	265	295
	INSTALLED Number of Drives Allocated + FORECAST Additional Drives	220	230	240	250	265	345	365	390	415	445	475
	INSTALLED - Total Drives Capacity	480	480	480	480	480	480	480	480	480	480	480
	INSTALLED - Total Drives Capacity @ 80% Threshold	384	384	384	384	384	384	384	384	384	384	384
	INSTALLED - Total Drives Capacity @70% (Recommnded)	336	336	336	336	336	336	336	336	336	336	336
	FORECAST - A2Z System unit Using All Drives (#)	1	1	1	1	1	1	1	1	1	1	1
	FORECAST - A2Z System unit with 80% Threshold (#)	1	1	1	1	1	1	1	2	2	2	2
	FORECAST - A2Z System unit with Recommended Threshold 70% (#)	1	1	1	1	1	2	2	2	2	2	2
File Count	FORECAST - A2Z System unit Based on File Count Limit	1	1	1	1	1	1	1	1	1	1	1

Figure 10.15a, can further be summarized thus:

- The forecast for additional disk is driven by I/O resource rather than storage space resource
- Additional A2Z system unit forecast from one unit to 2 units will first be required in Sept'17 (if the resource threshold usage level of 70% of the storage system is enforced) as shown in Figure 10.15c
- If the resource threshold usage level of 80% is to be used, the spending to install the additional A2Z system unit can be postponed for 2 months
- File count limit does not drive the need for additional A2Z storage system unit

Figure 10.15b forecast of A2Z storage system unit(s) – Resource type's

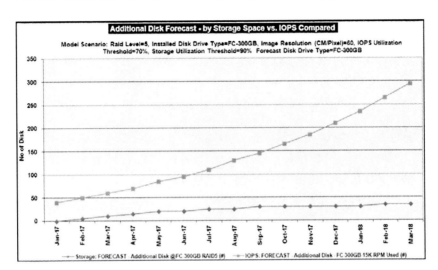

Figure 10.15c forecast of A2Z storage system unit(s) – graphical summary

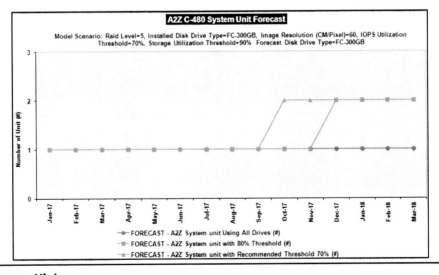

Success Hint:

When an IT system records a major incident with capacity as root cause, it calls for the capacity planning model to be revisited and refreshed. The model can be revalidated by comparing the actual vs. forecast and, if need be, the model can be recalibrated.

CAPACITY PLANNING FOR SHARED IT INFRASTRUCTURE RESOURCES

Shared IT infrastructure is the resources that are shared by two or more different IT services within an organization. Examples of shared infrastructure resources are: data centre, enterprise servers, enterprise grid, personal cloud, enterprise networks, enterprise storage, internet pipe, rack space, data centre space, grid cabinets, power system, cooling system, etc.

Typically, for each IT service most of the infrastructure resources forecast specified in the capacity plan will at implementation be provided through the data centre, and the associated shared infrastructures. Hence, it is important to have capacity plan for each of the shared infrastructure.

The capacity planning of each component of the shared infrastructure, should be driven by the sum total of the infrastructure resources' forecast, from all the dependent IT services; this serves as the demand forecast for shared infrastructure.

Usually, it takes more time to expand or increase the capacity of shared infrastructure components, consequently, for proactive capacity management, the planning should be based on long term forecast to allow enough time for implementation.

CRITICAL SUCCESS FACTORS FOR CAPACITY PLANNING MODEL

There are factors that are primary to building a reliable capacity planning model, these include:
- Accuracy of capacity planning model depends largely on the business demand forecast – a wrong business forecast will certainly lead to wrong

infrastructure forecast; and may result in excess or inadequate capacity for the IT service.

- Knowledge of the maximum business throughput volume an application or system can handle without performance degradation is vital, as it is the basis for determining when to add more capacity. Performance or single thread workload test can be helpful
- The use of data obtained through the most appropriate aggregation method, which retains the sustained peaks
- Using the metrics pair with good enough correlation/R-squared value
- Historical data (business, service and resource) collected using same timestamp
- Avoid the use of obsolete configuration value in model e.g. peak-to-average, transaction mix etc. These should be recalculated during each model refresh
- All throughput data should be normalized to use same timestamp and interval
- Having sufficient volume of historical data, as statistical accuracy depends on it

SUMMARY

Capacity risk can be triggered by the component of an IT system with the least available computing resources; in other words, IT system's capacity is equal to the component with the least capacity. The implication is that the capacity planning model, as a representation of real world IT system's performance, **must cover every component of the IT system**. Typical IT system components are web, application, database servers, storage, load balancers, networks, etc.

In modelling, it is important to be able to establish the mathematical relationship between any interdependent components' resource usage, in response to changing service/business demand.

Once the base model is working accurately, the model's "what if" options can then be used to predict various business scenarios. Models should be kept up to date by refreshing with the actual data, that is, replacing with more recent throughput, latency, and utilization data from the CDB.

ORGANIZATIONAL APPRAISAL

1. Do you currently have any model for your capacity planning?
2. For your critical applications, have you identified the system resource(s) causing performance bottleneck, specifically driving the performance of the individual applications?
3. Does your model focus on the critical system resource(s), causing performance bottleneck?
4. Is capacity planning model based on peak utilization?
5. Are the modelling assumptions communicated and agreed with the stakeholders?
6. Are your capacity planning models validated using "actual" versus "forecast" report?
7. Do you refresh your capacity planning model with recent data before use for new planning cycle?

11 CAPACITY PLANNING REVIEW WITH STAKEHOLDERS

"Quality is never an accident; it is always the result of high intention, sincere effort, intelligent direction and skilful execution"

– Willa A. Foster

INTRODUCTION

Technology users are not the end user of the capacity management process, but rather it is the business system owners of the IT systems or their representatives. The capacity management process is meant to help the application owner to realize the firm's objective; consequently, the application technical owners, support managers, and risk managers should be carried along with the capacity planning initiatives.

This review should focus on, among other things:

- o Validating the correctness of the historical business, service, and resource capacity CDB data used in the capacity planning model
- o Review and validate the capacity planning model built for the target IT service
- o This will help ensure that the stakeholders are involved in the capacity planning process, and not just rubber stamping the final capacity plan

REVIEW AUDIENCE

The more stakeholders involved in reviewing the model and proposed capacity plan. the better. The following should be in attendance: IT Technical owners, development team, support team, service level management and infrastructure team.

These stakeholders can provide and validate assumptions, as well as other information being used in the planning model

CAPACITY METRICS VALIDATION & DRAFT CAPACITY PLAN REVIEW

The application owners or their representative should periodically review the application's data collected by the monitoring tool, with a view to ensuring that the appropriate business and infrastructure metrics are collected.

This activity should initially be carried out when an application is first added to the capacity monitoring tool. Depending on the size of the organization's IT estate, metric validation process can be carried out in line with target application planning cycle, or at least annually.

Among the things to review as part of the validation process may include the following:
- Metrics collection covering all components of the application
- Confirm if there are new business capacity drivers/metrics that should be added to the monitoring tools collection
- Validate the existing metrics value for accuracy
- Validate the capacity value assigned to the business and service metrics
- Confirm if the appropriate aggregation methods are being applied

- Confirm that the service throughput metrics are collected at the appropriate sampling interval
- Verify that threshold breach alerting is configured, and with the appropriate threshold values.

CAPACITY PLANNING MODEL AND DRAFT CAPACITY FORECAST REVIEW

This focuses on reviewing the capacity planning model and the resultant capacity forecast with the stakeholders, before the publication of the formal capacity plan. The stakeholders should include the IT system owner, application support, infrastructure support, application architect and developers.

This is an evidential activity, to confirm that the target application has a capacity planning process reviewed and validated by the stakeholders, which provides the senior management the assurance that there will be adequate capacity to meet the current and future business demand at the right cost and time.

Prior to this review, the following should have occurred:
- The business user would have supplied their demand forecast data for the next planning period, typically one year forecast, to the capacity management team.
- The capacity management team, using the business supplied demand forecast data and the application's capacity planning model, would have produced a draft capacity plan
- Validate the accuracy of the capacity model, by reviewing the prior service and resource forecast versus the actual. Deviation of +/- 10% can be tolerated.

The review should also cover the following:
- Review and agree with the assumption of the capacity planning model, from which the capacity plan is produced
- Review and agree on the most cost efficient service improvement options
- Sign off on the draft capacity plan.

SUMMARY

For the capacity management process to be successfully implemented and deliver the expected benefits, the stakeholders must be carried along and actively participate in the capacity management review activities.

The business users or their representative should be involved in the capacity planning review activity; furthermore, they are expected to:
- Provide the business demand forecast
- Ensure that the right business metrics (driving capacity) are collected
- Validate the correctness of the business volume and throughput numbers published from the monitoring tool
- Validate the capacity planning model, and the business assumptions used in the model.

ORGANIZATIONAL APPRAISAL

1. With the aid of the configuration management database (CMDB) or other sources, do you know the key stakeholders for each IT services?
2. Are the key stakeholders (particularly the business system owners) involve in the capacity planning of their IT systems?

12 THE CAPACITY PLAN

"Plans are only good intentions unless they immediately degenerate into hard work"

- Peter Drucker.

WHAT IS CAPACITY PLAN?

Capacity plan is the key output of the capacity management process, and this is the output that mostly drives the process' ability to proactively manage capacity risks.

The capacity plan as it is called is a formal documented plan that needs to be verified for accuracy, reviewed, and acted upon by stakeholders. Capacity plan is a living document, which should be refreshed at least once within the business planning cycle; however, the organization's capacity management policy should clearly state the acceptable refresh period. Moreover, the refresh and review can also be driven by other predictable and non-predictable factors, like:

- New strategic business developments initiatives - acquisitions and takeovers
- Volatility of the business plan, in which case it can be refreshed quarterly
- Fast changing customer application usage behaviour e.g. change in service demand pattern, switching to new delivery channels
- Changes in technology or new technologies
- New products, new product channels or new shops/branches

177

- Seasonal festivities
- New marketing campaigns/promotions.

The capacity plan is an evidential document, which shows that capacity planning is undertaken as part of the capacity management process. Most of the information contained in the capacity plan comes from:

- Capacity planning "Inputs", discussed above in Table 9.1 of the "Capacity Planning" chapter, and
- The forecast information obtained at different levels, using the capacity planning model.

There should be capacity plan for each IT service; nevertheless, the individual IT systems/applications capacity plans can be combined into a single document as the enterprise capacity plan. The enterprise capacity plan provides a single financial outlook for budgeting purpose and regulatory compliance.

> **Success Hint:**
> Since the service and resource forecast information in the capacity plan are usually derived from the capacity planning model; it is important that the model is discussed, reviewed and validated by the stakeholders, particularly the business users.

CONTENTS OF A CAPACITY PLAN

Capacity plan is a reference document, often shared with internal and external stakeholders; it is expected to conform to the organizational agreed format.

Irrespective of the content format, based on good practice, certain key information is expected in the document.

Success Hint:

To help drive the quality of the information in a capacity plan, it is good that the organization adopts a capacity-plan-template. The template will help ensure; that the capacity plan for all IT services is consistent, and uniform.

Figure 12.1, shows the various key informational categories expected in a capacity plan; each is discussed further in detail.

Figure 12.1 Components of an IT Service capacity plan

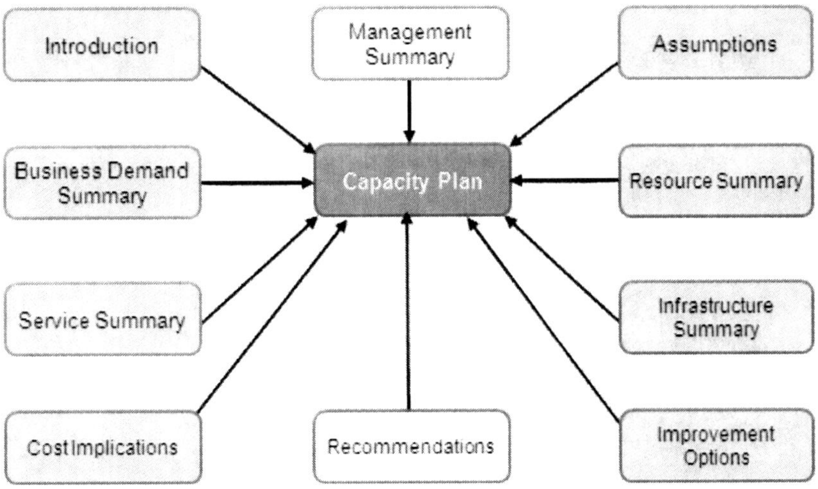

The Introduction

The introduction section is used to provide the background information, regarding the capacity plan for the target IT service. The following background information is expected as sub-sections:

Background

- Current level of capacity available to the target IT service, and how the SLA targets are being achieved
- The capacity risks being experienced due to insufficient capacity
- The avoidable cost being incurred from excess capacity
- What is new to the IT service in terms of capacity risks, and the associated consequences
- Changes that have occurred since the prior capacity plan was issued.

Scope of the plan

- State the IT infrastructures owned by the IT service, and its dependencies covered in the plan
- The in scope components should also be in compliance to the scope defined in the organization's capacity management process policy.

Methods used for information/data gathering and modelling

- State the source of historical business, service and resource data used
- State the source of the business demand forecast data; this further shows that the business is consulted
- State the forecasting method for arriving at the technical requests and resource forecasts (It is important that capacity model is discussed, reviewed and validated by the stakeholders).

Assumptions Made

- State all assumptions that have to hold for the capacity forecast to be valid with emphasis on the business assumptions e.g. Applications cumulative users does not account for lost users
- Some of the assumptions are used within the capacity planning model, this means that changing such will change the outcome of the model e.g. during the daily peak trading hour, 25% of the registered users will be using the application.

Management Summary

This can be a 1-3 pages of non technical summary for senior management. It should highlight the current or future capacity inadequacies and associated problems, the options, recommendation and cost implication.

Business Demand - Current & Forecast

- The Business demand is the key driver, it drives every other technical forecasts.
- The reason behind the new business demand forecast
- For the principal business capacity driver metric(s), state the recent historical and current business volume information - trends, monthly peaks, new all-time-high volume, since the last published capacity plan
- Present the business demand growth/contraction forecast for each of principal capacity driver metric(s), including the scenarios (e.g. optimistic, and pessimistic).

Service Summary - Current & Forecast Usage

- The details of the services that are covered by the plan
- The recent historical and current service volume information - trends, peak throughputs, peak latency, and the level at which SLA were met.

- Based on current demand forecast provided by the business, state the expected/forecast peak throughput, and latency for the respective services over the period covered by the plan.

Resource Summary - Current & Forecast Usage

- The details of the computing or infrastructure resource constituting performance bottleneck and driving capacity increase.
- Based on the summary of the service's recent historical, current throughputs, and latency, state the corresponding resource utilization information of the key system's resources - trends, average utilization, peak utilization and percentile level utilization.
- Based on current service forecast obtained from the capacity planning model or otherwise, state the expected/forecast peak resource utilization of the key resource metrics driving performance.

Infrastructure Summary - Scale up/down forecast

The resource utilization forecast stated in the resource summary section should be mapped to the specific physical infrastructure.

Depending on the resource type and application architecture, the resource forecast can be mapped to physical infrastructure like disk drive, memory, CPU, server, node, server cluster, storage system, etc. The infrastructure needs can also be about replacing the existing with the faster equivalent - faster disk, more CPU, faster CPU, Faster Network interface, etc.

Mapping the resource to physical infrastructure helps to broaden the options that can be used in the service improvement section.

Service Improvement Options

In this section, it is about making the most cost efficient decision towards meeting the business demand forecast within SLA. It can be:

- Findings ways to control or manage the resource utilization of the application, so as to minimize the additional infrastructure requirement. Among things to consider are:

    o Demand management – influence the use of computing resources via throughput reduction, pay back, batch and individual users volume reduction, restriction, and moving scheduled jobs to time of less resource demand (de-prioritizing non-critical users/operations during peak hours).
    o Performance tuning of application, middleware, database, workload balancing, etc.
    o Application redesign, to make data easily accessible to the CPU by storing data in hardware cache and RAM instead of disk.

- Choosing from the available upgrade paths using different physical infrastructure. For example, moving low utilization servers from physical servers to virtual servers.
- Choosing between implementing operational, tactical or strategic solution to the capacity upgrade need.

Cost Implications, and model

- Document the cost associated with the various options; the cost should include total cost of ownership.
- The fixed and recurring cost should be considered.
- Work towards ensuring compliance with organizational policy and procedure. Besides, the advice of the finance department can be solicited.

Recommendations

- To show management commitment to the capacity planning process, where applicable, the status of the recommendations from the prior capacity plan should be stated. Status can be stated as rejected, planned, partially implemented, fully implemented, etc.
- State the new recommendations, along with the proffered improvement options, and provide details as follows:
  - The risk being mitigated, and other benefits this will bring to the business
  - The capacity risks, and the potential impact of failing to implement the recommendations
  - The fixed and recurring cost needed to implement the recommendations; the cost is not limited to hardware, software, consultancy, personnel and labour
  - Where applicable, indicate the phased time-scale to spend for implementing the recommendations.

SUMMARY

The capacity plan is a formal document, and is the most important output of the capacity management process. It provides the key evidence that capacity is proactively planned for the current and future business demand.

The capacity management process is incomplete without a capacity plan; the implication is that service failures arising from capacity risk will mostly likely occur.

ORGANIZATIONAL APPRAISAL

1. Does your capacity plan get implemented?
2. Do you have capacity plan for each critical IT service, and the enterprise (consolidated) capacity plan that feed the IT budget?
3. Do the IT services capacity plans feed into the shared infrastructure and service capacity plan?

13 CAPACITY THRESHOLD ALERTING & RESPONSE TYPES

"Experience is not what happens to a man; it is what a man does
with what happens to him"

– Aldous Huxley.

INTRODUCTION

Threshold alerting is one of the iterative activities of the capacity management process, it is the rule by which the collected metrics data are examined and an alert is triggered if the specified threshold condition occurs.

The data examination for threshold breach can be in real-time, or through batch process that executes at predefined interval or during the daily aggregation run. Each of the methods has their pros and cons.

Very often, the real-time alerting is based on a single measurement; and hence has tendency to generate loads of alerts, which users tend to treat with levity as they may be assumed to be the usual false alarm. Consequently, real-time alerting should rather be used for very sensitive systems; where a threshold breached by just a single spike in measurement is considered critical. In order to mitigate against users getting flooded with alerts, the alerting mechanism should be set to trigger only after a specified number of threshold breaches occur within a specified interval.

On the contrary, threshold alerting generated through batch update can be tailored to use periodic aggregation value, to validate the threshold condition. As a result of using the aggregated value for threshold alert, the number of alerts generated is minimal, and alert can be suppressed for recurring threshold breaches.

Success Hint:

If the capacity management process is effective and proactive as it should be; then threshold alerting will be a warning sign for initiating the remediation of the pending capacity risk, and not a call for fire fighting.

WHAT IS THRESHOLD ALERTING

Threshold alerting is the utilization level of a capacity metric that is of significant interest; that the user wants to be notified of its occurrence. For example, a threshold alert can be set for the condition: disk storage "space used (%)" greater (>)70%.

Typically, a threshold alerting has three main parts:
- **The target metrics** e.g. "disk storage space used (%) "
- **The conditional operator** e.g. " greater (>)", and
- **The threshold value** e.g. "70%"

Conditional Operator
The conditional operator can be any of this, or a combination of them:
- Equal to (=)
- Greater than (>)

- Greater than or Equal to (>=)
- Less than (<)
- Less than or Equal to (<=)
- Between two values

Threshold Value

The threshold value is the metric value for determining when the threshold rule is met. The threshold value can be based on the metric's absolute measurement, periodic average of measurements, utilization (%), etc.

For threshold alert targeted towards mitigating capacity breaches, the threshold value is primarily determined by the lead time between the capacity upgrade initiation and completion time. For example:

- For additional disk storage allocation from SAN to a host, the threshold value can be set to 80%; as the host storage space capacity can be increased within 48 hours
- For a mobile messaging system for which capacity can only be increased or upgraded horizontally by adding new computer server cluster, the "active-users %usage" threshold value can be set at 70%; as it may take weeks to build and add new server cluster
- For a SAN system, the "IOPS %Usage" threshold value can be set to 60%; as it may take months to increase the SAN capacity either by upgrading or installing additional one.

CATEGORIES OF THRESHOLD ALERTING

There are different types of threshold alerting, which can be implemented using a capacity management tool. A threshold alert can simply be classified by its type and impact; as shown in Figure 13.1 (sample view from UnlimitedAnalytics software).

Figure 13.1 Threshold Alert Configuration Parameters

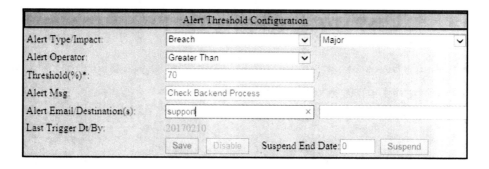

Alert Types

Each organization can define the alert types to suit her operation and information risk policy. Typical alert types are shown in Table 13.2:

Table 13.2   Alert Types

Type	Description
Breach	• This is for tracking alert caused by; capacity metrics measurement or utilization breaching the specified threshold. Alerts in this category, if not responded to, can lead to service performance degradation or failure. • It is worthy to note; that under utilization of system resource, or abnormally low metric value, should also be considered as breach. Threshold alert can be configured to track under utilization, through the use of the "Less than" alert operator.

Table 13.2 (continued)

Type	Description
New Record High	• This alert type is meant to draw attention to record high volumes in business volume, or even for a system resource. This threshold alert trigger each time a metric records a new value that is higher than the prior highest. • It is meant to draw the attention of stakeholders to increasing business activity. A "record high" alert type may not necessarily trigger a "Breach" alert type.

Data Quality	• This is information only alert, directed at the capacity management team and data-source provider; it is meant to uncover data quality issues with metrics that needs to be regularized.
	
	• Examples of data quality issues include:
	    o A metric designed to have 100% maximum usage, having a percentage usage value that is greater than 100%
	    o When a business metric's absolute measurement value is greater than the specified absolute capacity value
	    o When a resource or business metric's measurement, that is never expected to be zero; sends zero or negative values to the CDB.

Alert Impact

In practice, it is good to associate a threshold alerting with a specific risk impact level. The impact level is a measure of the risk consequences the organization will likely be exposed to if the threshold breach is not managed.

Alert Impact classification varies, but typically can include:
- Severe
- Major
- Minor,
- Information Only,
- None

ALERT MESSAGES

Capacity management threshold alert breach messages can be delivered to the recipients using different mix of channels. Among the common channels are emails and SMS. Furthermore, the alert action can be integrated into the organization's service management system, to raise incident ticket.

Raising incident ticket, via integration with the firm's service management system; is one of the most effective ways to ensure that capacity management threshold alerting is given the adequate attention it requires. The ticket, once opened in the incident system, will most likely be closed only after the assigned-user has effectively managed the alerted risk. Unlike email or SMS, as long as the raised ticket remains open or pending, it will continue to get attention or be reassigned, or escalated.

Capacity management alert messages should provide the details that ought to make it easy to know the specific source of the alert, and the threshold rule that is breached. Typical capacity alert emails are presented in Figure 13.3 (from the UnlimitedAnalytics capacity management tool).

Figure 13.3a Capacity Management Email Alert

UnlimitedAnalytics	iDemo Bizd Ltd - UK
Metrics Threshold Notification	
One of the metrics has breached its threshold in UnlimitedAnalytics	
Metrics Details	
Date	20170210 221804
Event	Breached: Usage >= 90% on 20170210 135558
Data Source	Balancesheet
Metric Name	Accounts Payable Transactions per hour (Trans count in Mils)
Age Type	Hour
Aggregation Type	Count
Host/Data Set	UK Plant
Row Filter	Transition Bucket
Column Filter	All
Metric Value	Value: 901
Metric Capacity	Capacity: 1000
Usage	Usage: 90.10%

Figure 13.3b Capacity Management Email Alert

UnlimitedAnalytics	iDemo Bizd Ltd - UK
Metrics Threshold Notification	
One of the metrics has breached its threshold in UnlimitedAnalytics	
Metrics Details	
Date	20170210 221804
Event	Breached: Usage > 50% on 20170210 123059
Data Source	DeviceActivationSystem
Metric Name	Average Latency (msec)
Age Type	Hour
Aggregation Type	Average
Host/Data Set	All
Row Filter	EMEA
Column Filter	Nokia8
Metric Value	Value: 6.5
Metric Capacity	Capacity: 10
Usage	Usage: 65%

Characteristically, it should provide the following vital information:

- RAG based colour, to indicate the risk impact of the reported breach
- The data source and the specific metric that was breached
- The breached threshold condition
- Date-time the breach occurred, and the date-time it was reported

---

Success Hint:

Capacity management alerts arising from threshold breach are best handled by having an incident ticket raised for them. As much as possible, this activity should be automatic through integration with the IT service management incident system.

SUMMARY

Threshold alerting is a key functionality expected from any capacity monitoring tool. Threshold alerting can be either proactive or reactive, depending on the set threshold values. Threshold values should be set to allow for time to fully mitigate the risk associated with the alert.

For threshold alerting to be useful, the following should be noted:

- Alert messages should contain details of the metric's name and measurement, the breached threshold, and the alert condition.
- Alert messages should be sent to user groups, instead of individual users
- Alert messages can have higher probability of being attended to if it is integrated with the service management application; to automatically raise incident.
- The number of alert messages each day should be minimal.

- The alert messages should not be too frequent, as they will often get ignored

ORGANIZATIONAL APPRAISAL

1. Do you have capacity utilization threshold alerting implemented for both infrastructure resources and business metrics?
2. Is the volume of threshold breach alerting controlled so as to avoid alerting flood which is treated with levity at risk of missing critical alert messages?
3. Are the alert responses for both infrastructures resources and business metrics handled separately as the response actions for both may be different?
4. Towards ensuring proper response to alerting messages, is your capacity management system integrated with the IT service management incident system?

14 CLOUD COMPUTING CAPACITY MANAGEMENT

"As long as computing resources are limited in supply and obtained at a cost, there will always be capacity planning"

– Dominic Ogbonna (the author)

INTRODUCTION

Cloud computing is a typical term for an internet-based delivery of computing services which offers online access to computer services or resources.

There are three **types of clouds**, namely:

- **Public** - the cloud providers make computing resources and services available to the customers/clients over the internet. Customer data is stored at a data centre owned and managed by the cloud computing providers.

- **Private** - similar to public, but the data and services are provided behind firewall owned by the customer. The implication is that the customers/organization using private cloud, have major control over the management and security of the infrastructure.

- **Hybrid** - a combination of both the public and private cloud. The customer's organizational policy, regulatory, and industry requirements are applied to determine which cloud type will host any particular IT systems.

Additionally, the common **cloud service models** are namely:

- **SaaS** (Software as a Service) - this cloud service model offers applications to end-users. The users of SaaS based applications do not need to bother about maintaining the IT system, or managing the infrastructure, as these are taken care of by the service provider. However, the user is empowered with the administrative privileges to manage the applications e.g. create other end-users, allocate limits to users, etc. The SaaS provider offers same software to all users, with little or no aesthetics customization.

- **PaaS** (Platform as a Service) - for this cloud service model, the cloud service provider provides and manages the platform (infrastructure resources, databases, email, load balancing, messaging queues, email, etc.) required by the users/customers to build their applications. This model helps the customers to focus on their core objective of building and supporting application.

- **IaaS** (Infrastructure as a Service) - within this cloud model, the users are provided with raw computing, storage, network infrastructure, and the capability to provision them on-demand. It provides users with highest level of administrative control of their enterprise IT resources. The IaaS service model provides users with the same traditional IT infrastructure estate, except that the infrastructure belongs to a cloud service provider.

Doing your business through the cloud does not invalidate any of the 3 sub processes of the capacity management process, as:

- Business: demand of IT services still emanates from the users/customers
- Service: the need to measure service performance and throughput, operating within SLA, remains
- Resource: technology services and applications will still need to be hosted on virtual/physical infrastructure, from where they will draw resources, and these resources are always obtained at a cost.

Cloud computing is about providing computing resource. So the question is, "do cloud computing providers have infinite computing resources to meet the current and future demand of their customers?" The answer is likely to be "No!". Consequently, these cloud computing resource providers will also need to manage their capacity. In other words, the capacity management process is still relevant and ongoing, but the responsibility may shift from one entity to another.

CLOUD COMPUTING CAPACITY MANAGEMENT - THE OPEN QUESTIONS

- What amount of historical data will be kept by the non-IaaS providers? Amazon® Web Services monitoring service - CloudWatch® probably keeps about 18 months of data.
- The cloud computing monitoring is more focused on infrastructure resource utilization. The providers will need to provide flexible and robust service, for publishing custom business data where the granularity requirement is in seconds and not minutes.
- The Amazon's "Reserved Instance Marketplace" (where users of EC2® can sell excess purchased computing capacity) is an indication that capacity management should not be relaxed.
- In the cloud, there will be tendency to ignore the traditional capacity planning improvement options to explore the most cost efficient way to manage resource usage and end up just adding server.
- Deploying application with poor and inefficient code (for example, getting cpu bound at 40% utilization) on a burst trading day could cause the business to incur much cost, as tens/hundreds of servers may be added on demand.
- The aim of good application is to drive the CPU utilization as high as possible, without impacting SLA (but not sustained at high utilization). If this is

the case, then automatic addition of computing resource via on-demand model should be driven by service throughput and latency, and not resource utilization. Else, cloud customers may be penalized for running resource-efficient applications that maximize the CPU resource.

- When will organizations muster the courage and confidence to migrate their mission-critical legacy mainframe applications (running on DB2 and Sybase database servers that not commonly provided in PaaS, and IaaS) to the cloud? Partial migration will create a situation; where capacity is managed on two fronts – which can be likened to a football match where there are two goal keepers manning one post (will the two save or concede more goals?).

- In the long run, organizations may need to review the cost incurred from the on-demand capacity of adding resources instantly (usually at higher prices), and reconsider if traditional capacity planning will be used to forecast future resources needs, and have them purchased at normal rate.

CLOUD COMPUTING CAPACITY MANAGEMENT – WHAT TO EXPECT

As cloud computing gain more ground and acceptability as it is expected the big clients and consumers will demand more control of capacity, towards reducing cloud charges. It is very likely cloud computing service providers will offer the basic requirements at no extra charge; but charge consumers for non-basic services. Therefore, it should be anticipated that almost every activity within the capacity management process may end up being offered as chargeable cloud services. The likely future chargeable capacity management process based cloud services are:

- CapacityMonitoring-as-a-Service
- CapacityAlerting-as-a-Service

- CapacityResourceDataCollection-as-a-Service
- CapacityBusinessDataCollection-as-a-Service
- CapacityDataStorage-as-a-Service
- CapacityDataAggregation-as-a-Service
- CapacityDataAnalysis -as-a-Service
- CapacityReporting-as-a-Service
- CapacityModelling-as-a-Service
- CapacityPlanning-as-a-Service
- CapacityPlanDocument-as-a-Service
- CapacityRootCauseAnalysis-as-a-Service

Success Hint:

In cloud computing, the goal of capacity management has not changed, rather, the responsibility may theoretically shifted to or practically shared with the cloud service provider.

CAPACITY MANAGEMENT IN MACHINE LEARNING ERA

Even as the then buzz word "Cloud Computing" has become a reality, so also, the latest computing buzz word "Machine Learning" (ML) and its potentials in capacity management should not be discarded with a wave of hand. Rather, machine learning method offers data analysis potentials that could help with the automation of analytical capacity planning models.

The term "Machine Learning" was coined by Arthur Samuel in 1959 while at IBM. The machine learning concept is aimed at getting computers to learn without being programmed to do so, with the objective of providing feedback-information needed for decision making.

There are about three main categories of machine learning methods, namely:

- Supervised learning
- Unsupervised learning
- Reinforcement learning.

Associated with the above categories are several machine learning algorithms that are ever increasing. One or more of the algorithms working together can be applied to resolve some of the iterative activities of the capacity management process.

SUMMARY

According to Hegel, "History teaches that history teaches us nothing". Furthermore, the 1940s invention of semiconductor devices made it possible to produce solid-state device, which were considerably smaller, more efficient, more cheaper, more reliable, and more durable; which eventually replaced vacuum tubes. Comparatively, the cloud computing is a force that may eventually swallow up other infrastructure strategy.

However, capacity management process, and capacity planning may never become obsolete, as the process is still required to cost effectively manage computing resources. We will likely see a shift of the capacity planning responsibility between cloud computing service providers, and users.

In cloud computing, one thing that would remain guaranteed is having adequate resource through on-demand capacity, but what would not be remain guaranteed is cost of the on-demand capacity. It is this cost element that would eventually determine if cloud users will return to the traditional capacity planning.

Finally, let us remember that one other objective of the capacity management process is reducing the cost of doing business through:

- Cost reduction by avoiding panic buying: cloud computing on-demand capacity can be likened to panic buying.
- Cost reduction by eliminating computing resource over-provisioning: in cloud computing, to avoid the "expensive" on-demand capacity, customers will end up over-provisioning.

ORGANIZATIONAL APPRAISAL

1. Do you have a post cloud computing adoption strategy, for capacity management?
2. In cloud computing, how do you ensure there is no excess resource provisioning?
3. In cloud computing, how do you decide when to activate the on-demand capacity increase?
4. Have you started considering the use of machine learning to aid your capacity management functions?

15 AUDITING THE CAPACITY MANAGEMENT PROCESS

"The only real mistake is the one from which we learn nothing"

- John Powell

INTRODUCTION

Capacity management process auditing is aimed at providing an independent review of an organization's policies, procedures and standards for ensuring that the capacity management process is effective. This ensures that the process can provide the assurance that there is adequate infrastructure and computing resources to cope with the current and future business demand of the organization.

The auditing process can be conducted to fulfil internal, external or regulatory compliance. The regulatory compliance type depends on the organization's operating business sector. If the internal audit of the capacity management process is comprehensively and effectively conducted, then it is expected that it can also comply with the compliance requirements of both the external and regulatory teams.

KEY CONTROL OBJECTIVES

The objective of a capacity management process audit is to:

Assess the readiness and effectiveness of controls designed and implemented for the capacity management process. Additionally, it provides the assurance that the organization's IT systems can support the current and future business demand cost effectively, and in a timely manner.

SCOPE

The capacity management process audit should be focused on the process' components and the controls implemented; to ensure support for the control's objective. Amongst the components for auditing are:

- Availability of policy and procedures guiding the implementation of the capacity management process, and when last they are updated
- Criteria for determining which systems and infrastructure should be covered by the capacity management process
- Stakeholder involvement in capacity management process, and their roles. The identified process ownership, management and management committees.
- Verify that all tiers/components of an IT systems, e.g. web servers, application servers, database servers, etc. are adequately covered by the capacity management process, including capacity planning activities
- Verify that monitoring, collection of business volumetric and infrastructure performance data are in place for all IT assets meant to be covered by the capacity management process
- Generally ensure that the capacity management process is in line with the firm's capacity management policy and procedures

- Ensuring that collected business data does not include clients private detail or any confidential information, as this may be against the host country data protection law
- Capacity management data storage, aggregation, and analysis
- Capacity management reporting, and capacity plan
- Personnel adequacy, for supporting the capacity management process functions.

CONTROL REQUIREMENTS

Based on the scope, the control requirements listed in Table 15.1 can be used to audit the capacity management process. This control requirement can apply at organizational/firm level or IT systems level (specific to those in scope).

Table 15.1 Audit Control Requirements

Control Requirements	Apply To
Evidence of approved and published capacity management process policy document	Firm level
Evidence of approved and published capacity management process procedure document	Firm level
Evidence of capacity management process steering committee meetings	Firm level
Evidence of monitoring - published and distributed monthly capacity reports (business metrics focused), for all IT systems covered by the capacity management process	Firm level

Table 15.1   (continued)

Control Requirements	Apply To
Evidence that the service level agreement (SLA) with third Party IT service providers covers capacity, performance monitoring, and reporting	Firm level
Evidence that all capacity risk caused service incidents have been addressed.	Firm level
Evidence that the capacity metrics (business, service, and resource) are collected, stored, and available for historical analysis and reporting	Firm level
The current and business driven capacity plan	IT Service
Evidence that the IT service plan is reviewed with stakeholders, and acted upon	IT Service
Evidence that all dependent IT services/components are covered by the capacity plan	IT Service
Appropriate method is used in determining the capacity limit of business metrics, if not based on performance testing	IT Service
Where applicable, evidence that performance testing is carried out	IT Service
Evidence of business plan from the business that serves as input to the capacity plan	IT Service

Table 15.1 (continued)

Control Requirements	Apply To
proof that business users periodically review and validate the collected business metrics and the capacity limits	IT Service
Capacity plan implementation proof	IT Service
Evidence that threshold alerting is implemented and acted upon when triggered	IT Service

SUMMARY

The capacity management process like other business processes necessary for meeting the business goal, should be audited, to ensure the process expectations and standards are met.

The capacity management process should be audited regularly, based on the organization's predetermined interval with a view to determining the following:

- That the capacity management process adheres to the organization's capacity management strategy and procedure.
- Ensure the process evidentially meets the regulatory requirements

ORGANIZATIONAL APPRAISAL

1. Does your capacity management policy, specify the control requirements for determining compliance of an IT service.

2. Do the firm's risks/audit teams carry out capacity management process compliance check for the individual IT services?

3. Does your capacity management system implementation provide functionality that provides visibility to the compliance level for each on-boarded IT service?

APPENDIX A – UNIX: PERFORMANCE DATA COLLECTION TECHNIQUES

INTRODUCTION

The Unix operating system and its variants e.g. Linux has an inbuilt utility, for performance monitoring of the provided resources. Amongst the Unix resources monitored are CPU, memory, disk space, input/output time, network time, etc.

Unix and its variants provide many command-line utilities for monitoring and collecting the performance of the various resource types. In this book only vmstat, sar, and iostat will be discussed.

VMSTAT UTILITY

Description
- vmstat reports information processes, memory, paging, block I/O, traps and CPU activities
- The reports are intended to help identify system bottlenecks. Also, note that Linux vmstat does not count itself as a running process.

Manual

The usage detail of the vmstat utility can be obtained by executing the command below from the Unix command-line:

man vmstat

Usage

The vmstat comes with many options, but for basic monitoring use the command:

*vmstat -n -S K [**delay** [**count**]]*

-n causes the header not to be reprinted /displayed repeatedly, but just once

-S unit size, must be followed by the (k, K, m, or M options which represent 1000, 1024, 1000000, and 1048576 respectively), the default is K.

delay the delay between updates in seconds. If no delay is specified, only one report is printed; with the average values since boot.

count specifies the number of times that the statistics are repeated

Command Output Sample

For the command:

vmstat 30 2

The output looks thus:

```
procs -----------memory---------- ---swap-- -----io---- --system-- -----cpu------
 r  b   swpd   free   buff    cache   si   so    bi   bo    in   cs   us sy id wa st
 3  0      0 7447508 305700 13213852    0    0     6   33     2   32   17  3 80  0  0
 3  0      0 7395768 305700 13214864    0    0     0  336 15652 16557  43 13 44  0  0
 3  0      0 7395888 305700 13214900    0    0     0  336 15652 16557  45 11 44  0  0
```

Field Descriptions

As described in source (man vmstat):

Procs

r: The number of processes waiting for run time.

b: The number of processes in uninterruptible sleep.

Memory

swpd: the amount of virtual memory used.

free: the amount of idle memory.

buff: the amount of memory used as buffers.

cache: the amount of memory used as cache.

inact: the amount of inactive memory. (-a option)

active: the amount of active memory. (-a option)

Swap

si: Amount of memory swapped in, from disk (/s).

so: Amount of memory swapped to disk (/s).

IO

bi: Blocks received from a block device (blocks/s).

bo: Blocks sent to a block device (blocks/s).

System

in: The number of interrupts per second, including the clock.

cs: The number of context switches per second.

CPU

These are percentages of the total CPU time.

us: Time spent running non-kernel code. (user time, including nice time)

sy: Time spent running kernel code. (system time)

id: Time spent idle. Prior to Linux 2.5.41, this includes IO-wait time.

wa: Time spent waiting for IO. Prior to Linux 2.5.41, included in idle.

st: Time stolen from a virtual machine. Prior to Linux 2.6.11, unknown.

Formatting vmstat as CSV data-source for CDB feed

The script displayed below can be saved in file, and the script executed each time the server boots. The script saves the output of the vmstat as hourly CSV file; and adds the date, time, and the server's hostname to every record.

Modify the script's delay time of 30 seconds to suit your environment; and the output file, named as applicable.

213

Unix Script in a file:

```
ofile=`hostname`+vmstat_`date '+%Y%m%d%H'`.csv
echo "Date,Time,Hostname,r,b,swpd,free,buff,cache,si,so,bi,bo,in,cs,us,sy,id,wa,st"
>> $ofile
vmstat 30 -n -S K | while read line; do
        echo `date -u ' + %Y-%m-%d:%M:%S'` `hostname` "$line" | grep -v -e free -
e memory | awk '{{for(n=1;n<NF;n++) {printf "%s,",$n} {print $NF}}}' >>        $ofile
done
```

Script Sample Output:

```
Date,Time,Hostname,r,b,swpd,free,buff,cache,si,so,bi,bo,in,cs,us,sy,id,wa,st
2016-12-30,16:32:00,5ss01_app1_db01,3,0,0,7447508,305700,13213852,0,0,6,33,2,32,17,3,80,0,0
2016-12-30,16:32:30,5ss01_app1_db01,3,0,0,7395768,305700,13214864,0,0,0,336,15652,16557,43,13,44,0,0
2016-12-30,16:33:00,5ss01_app1_db01,3,0,0,7395888,305700,13214900,0,0,0,336,15652,16557,45,11,44,0,0
```

Note, vmstat manual recommends excluding the first record from use.

SAR UTILITY

sar - Collect, report, or save system activity information.

Synopsis

sar [-A] [-b] [-B] [-C] [-d] [-h] [-i interval] [-m] [-p] [-q] [-r] [-R] [-S] [-t] [-u [ALL]] [-v] [-V] [-w] [-W] [-y] [-j { ID | LABEL | PATH | UUID | ... }] [-n { keyword [,...] | ALL }] [-I { int [,...] | SUM | ALL | XALL }] [-P { cpu [,...] | ALL }] [-o [filename] | -f [filename]] [--legacy] [-s [hh:mm:ss]] [-e [hh:mm:ss]] [interval [count]]

Description

The usage detail of the sar utility can be obtained by executing the command below from the Unix command-line:

man sar

The sar has vast amount of reports to offer across many system resources, but the book will be considering how it is used for monitoring some key resource types, namely: CPU; memory; I/O and transfer; and paging stats.

Formatting vmstat as CSV data-source for CDB feed

The script shown below can be saved in a file, and the script executed each time the server boots. The script saves the output of the sar as hourly CSV file; and adds the date, server's hostname to every record.

Modify the script's delay time of 30 seconds, to suit your environment; and the output file, named as desired.

1. CPU Performance Metrics

Unix Script in a file:

```
ofile=`hostname`_sar_cpu_`date '+%Y%m%d%H'`.csv
echo
"Date,Hostname,Time,CpuName,%user,%nice,%system,%iowait,%steal,%idle,null"
>> $ofile
sar -u 30 | while read line; do
        echo `date -u '+ %Y-%m-%d'` `hostname` "$line" | grep ":" | grep -v -e CPU
-e      average -e % -e / | tr "\n" "" | awk  -F "" ' BEGIN{OFS=","} {{for(n=1; n<=NF;
n++)    { printf "%s,",$n} ;  printf "\n'} ' >>        $ofile
done
```

Script Sample Output:

```
Date,Hostname,Time,CpuName,%user,%nice,%system,%iowait,%steal,%idle,null
2016-12-30,u5ss01_core01,17:48:00,all,1.43,0.00,0.68,0.35,0.00,97.55,
2016-12-30,u5ss01_core01,17:48:30,all,0.95,0.00,0.65,1.43,0.00,96.97,
2016-12-30,u5ss01_core01,17:49:00,all,1.25,0.03,0.38,0.80,0.00,97.55,
```

2. Memory Performance Metrics

Unix Script in a file:

```
ofile=`hostname`_sar_mem_`date '+%Y%m%d%H'`.csv
echo
"Date,Hostname,Time,kbmemfree,kbmemused,%memused,kbbuffers,kbcached,kb
commit,%commit,null" >> $ofile
sar -r 30 | while read line; do
        echo `date -u '+ %Y-%m-%d'` `hostname` "$line" | grep ":" | grep -v -e CPU
-e      average -e % -e / | tr "\n" "" | awk -F "" ' BEGIN{OFS=","} {{for(n=1; n<=NF;
n++)    { printf "%s,",$n} ; printf "\n"} ' >>        $ofile
done
```

Script Sample Output:

```
Date,Hostname,Time,kbmemfree,kbmemused,%memused,kbbuffers,kbcached,kbcommit,%commit,null
2016-12-30,u5ss01_core01,17:48:00,18441340,14436640,43.91,1050628,6103328,9850108,23.87,
2016-12-30,u5ss01_core01,17:48:30,18443348,14434632,43.90,1050628,6104672,9846596,23.86,
2016-12-30,u5ss01_core01,17:49:00,18444000,14433980,43.90,1050628,6104680,9841212,23.84,
```

3. I/O and Transfer Performance Metrics

Unix Script in a file:

```
ofile=`hostname`_sar_io_`date '+%Y%m%d%H'`.csv
echo "Date,Hostname,Time,tps,rpts,wtps,bread/s,bwrtn/s,null" >> $ofile
sar -b 30 | while read line; do
        echo `date -u '+ %Y-%m-%d'` `hostname` "$line" | grep ":" | grep -v -e CPU
-e      average -e % -e / | tr "\n" "" | awk -F "" ' BEGIN{OFS=","} {{for(n=1; n<=NF;
n++)    { printf "%s,",$n} ; printf "\n"} ' >>        $ofile
done
```

Script Sample Output:

```
Date,Hostname,Time,tps,rpts,wtps,bread/s,bwrtn/s,null
2016-12-30,u5ss01_core01,17:01:30,4.20,0.00,4.20,0.00,116.80,
2016-12-30,u5ss01_core01,17:02:00,6.61,0.00,6.61,0.00,153.91,
2016-12-30,u5ss01_core01,17:02:30,5.62,0.00,5.62,0.00,97399,
```

4. Paging Performance Metrics

Unix Script in a file:

*ofile=`hostname`_**sar_paging**_`date '+%Y%m%d%H'`.csv*
echo
*"**Date,Hostname,Time,pgpgin/s,pgpgout/s,fault/s,majflt/s,pgscank/s,pgsteal/s,%vm eff,null** >> $ofile*
*sar -B **30** | while read line; do*
    echo `date -u '+ %Y-%m-%d'` `hostname` "$line" | grep ":" | grep -v -e CPU
-e   average -e % -e / | tr "\n" "" | awk -F "" ' BEGIN{OFS=","} {{for(n=1; n<=NF;
n++)   { printf "%s,",$n} ; printf "\n'} ' >> $ofile
done

Script Sample Output:

```
Date,Hostname,Time,pgpgin/s,pgpgout/s,fault/s,majflt/s,pgscank/s,pgsteal/s,%vmeff,null
2016-12-30,u5ss01_core01,17:55:21,0.00,50.30,2057.68,0.00,1496.01,0.00,0.00,0.00,0.00,
2016-12-30,u5ss01_core01,17:55:51,0.00,37.68,3290.98,0.00,2546.89,0.00,0.00,0.00,0.00,
2016-12-30,u5ss01_core01,17:56:21,0.00,52.10,2562.73,0.00,1823.45,0.00,0.00,0.00,0.00,
```

IOSTAT UTILITY

Description

- iostat reports CPU statistics, and I/O statistics for devices and partitions; information processes, memory, paging, block I/O, traps and CPU activity.
- The performance metrics are intended to help identify system bottlenecks.

Manual

The usage detail of the iostat utility can be obtained by executing the command below from the Unix command-line:

man iostat

APPENDIX B - WINDOWS: PERFORMANCE DATA COLLECTION TECHNIQUES

Introduction

Windows operating system provides many inbuilt functions/tools for monitoring and collecting the system resource performance data. However, among the command-line utilities, the LOGMAN.EXE utility seems to be the most robust, flexible, easy to use, and designed for automated data collections. LOGMAN.EXE is not designed to provide data visualization, but data files; that can be fed into your CDB for aggregation, analysis, and reporting.

Besides performance data collection, the logman.exe has other functionalities. For the detailed use of logman.exe, from your windows command-line prompt, type "logman.exe /?" and press the enter key. If the command fails, search for logman.exe file in system32 directory

LOGMAN.EXE

Logman.exe Syntax

As described in source (longman.exe /?):

Usage:
  logman.exe [create | query | start | stop | delete | update | import | export] [options]

Verbs:
  create -   Create a new data collector.
  query - Query data collector properties. If no name is given, all data collectors
are listed.

start - Start an existing data collector and set the begin time to manual.
stop - Stop an existing data collector and set the end time to manual.
delete - Delete an existing data collector.
update - Update an existing data collector's properties.
import - Import a data collector set, from an XML file.
export - Export a data collector set, to an XML file.

Adverbs:
counter - Create a counter data collector.
trace - Create a trace data collector.
alert - Create an alert data collector.
cfg -Create a configuration data collector.

Options (counter):
Options: run "logman.exe /?" command for help details.

Using Logman.exe for performance data collection

Step #1:

Create a PerfMon counter definition file, including all windows performance counters you want collected. The counter file used is named: **winperf_key_counters.cfg**. The content is shown below containing only two metric categories, more can be added:

\Memory\Available MBytes

\Processor(_Total)*

Step #2:

Create a new PerfMon data collector, on the target server; using the counter file "winperf_key_counters.cfg" created in step #1, use the single line command:

logman.exe create counter ***winperf_key_log*** *-v mmddhhmm -max* ***250*** *-cf* ***\\<Your CDB server>\\perflogs\winperf_key_counters.cfg*** *-si* ***00:00:30*** *-cnf* ***01:00:00*** *-f csv -o \\<Your CDB* ***server>\perflogs\%computername%_perfdata.csv***

Command Options Meaning:

- -v {nnnnnn | mmddhhmm}

Attach file versioning information, to the end of the log name. When the "mmddhhmm" option is used, this will append the file creation date and time to the end of the performance data file, e.g. winperf_key_data_5SS10_**07172249**.csv.

- -max value

Specifies the maximum log file size, in MB or number of records for SQL logs.

- -cf filename

File listing performance counters to collect, one per line. In the example, the performance counter file is winperf_key_counters.cfg which is remotely located, this makes it easy to change the counter, and uniform counters collected across all servers.

- -si [[hh:]mm:]ss

Sample interval for performance counter data collectors. For example, "00:00:30" collects performance data every 30 seconds.

- -cnf [[hh:]mm:]ss

Create a new file when the specified time has elapsed or when the max size is exceeded. For example, "01:00:00" implies that a new file should be created every hour.

- -f {bin | bincirc | csv | tsv | sql}

The log format for the data collector, the option "csv" means; the data should be saved in csv format.

- -o {path | dsn!log}

Path of the output log file or the DSN and log set name in a SQL database.

The used option: "*<Your CDB server>*\perflogs\%computername%_perfdata.csv" is broken down as:

\\<Your CDB server>\perflogs\: data files are saved in a central remote location, from where the data will be uploaded to the CDB. Additionally, collected performance data will not be lost, even if the monitored server crashes.

%computername%: this adds the target server hostname as part of the filename; which can be used for identifying different servers, at the point of uploading the data to the CDB.

Step #3:

In the manual mode, start the data collector using this command:

logman.exe start ***winperf_key_log***

Alternatively, the automatic mode, the "-b" and the "-e" options should be included when creating the PerfMon collector in step #2 above. This command kicks off the performance data generation, into the designated output log file.

Step #4:

In the manual mode, start the data collector using this command:

logman.exe stop ***winperf_key_log***

Step #5:

Delete an existing data collector created in step #2, using this command:

logman.exe delete ***winperf_key_log***

Output from the collection

Figure A.1, shows the output file content for the PerfMon data, collected using the Logman.exe Windows utility. Always ensure the first record is not included in your data ingestion to CDB or analysis.

Figure B.1 Windows PerfMon - Output File Content

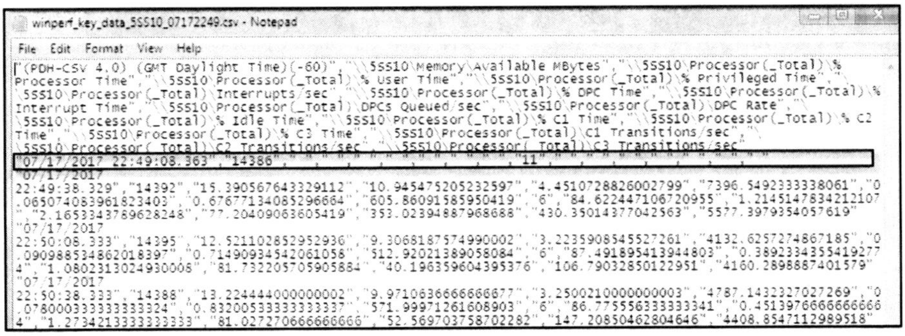

```
winperf_key_data_5SS10_07172249.csv - Notepad
File  Edit  Format  View  Help
"(PDH-CSV 4.0) (GMT Daylight Time)(-60)","\\5SS10\Memory\Available MBytes","\\5SS10\Processor(_Total)\%
Processor Time","\\5SS10\Processor(_Total)\% User Time","\\5SS10\Processor(_Total)\% Privileged Time","\
\5SS10\Processor(_Total)\Interrupts/sec","\\5SS10\Processor(_Total)\% DPC Time","\\5SS10\Processor(_Total)\%
Interrupt Time","\\5SS10\Processor(_Total)\DPCs Queued/sec","\\5SS10\Processor(_Total)\DPC Rate","\
\5SS10\Processor(_Total)\% Idle Time","\\5SS10\Processor(_Total)\% C1 Time","\\5SS10\Processor(_Total)\% C2
Time","\\5SS10\Processor(_Total)\% C3 Time","\\5SS10\Processor(_Total)\C1 Transitions/sec","\
\5SS10\Processor(_Total)\C2 Transitions/sec","\\5SS10\Processor(_Total)\C3 Transitions/sec"
"07/17/2017 22:49:08.363","14386"," "," "," "," "," "," "," ","11"," "," "," "," "," "," "," "
"07/17/2017
22:49:38.329","14392","15.390567643329112","10.945475205232597","4.4510728826002799","7396.5492333338061","0
.0650740839618234 03","0.67677134085296664","605.86091585950419","6","84.622447106720955","1.214514783421210 7
","2.16533437896282 48","77.20409063605419","353.02394887968688","430.35014377042563","5577.3979354057619"
"07/17/2017
22:50:08.333","14395","12.521102852952936","9.3068187574990002","3.2235908545527261","4132.6257274867185","0
.090988534862018397","0.7149093454206105 8","512.92021389058084","6","87.491895413944803","0.389233435541927 7
4","1.0802313024930008","81.732205705905884","40.196359604395376","106.79032850122951","4160.2898887401579"
"07/17/2017
22:50:38.333","14388","13.224444000000002","9.9710636666666677","3.2500210000000003","4787.1432327027269","0
.078000333333333324","0.83200533333333337","571.99971261608903","6","86.775556333333341","0.451397666666666 6
4","1.2734213333333333","81.027270666666666","52.569703758702282","147.20850462804646","4408.8547112989518"
```

> ***Success Hint:***
>
> As a rule, when uploading PerfMon data to CDB, always skip the first data record as most often the field values are wrong, and can adversely affect average, and minimum aggregated values.

Other Performance Counters:

In addition to the counters defined in step #1, more counters are listed below, and each can be further qualified to narrow down to required specifics:

\LogicalDisk(*)*

\Memory*

\Network Interface(*)*

\Paging File(*)*

\PhysicalDisk(*)*

\Process(*)*

\Redirector*

\Server*

\System*

\Thread(*)*

> **Success Hint:**
>
> Windows PerfMon data record is formatted as variable columnar data (adding new counters can shift metric position in the data file), therefore, data parsing script or the CDB; should have the functionality to support moving column data.

GLOSSARY OF TERMS

Analytical Modelling A prediction technique that uses mathematical models.

Application A software program hosted by an information system to perform a specific function.

Auxiliary Business Metrics A term introduced in this book for describing non-principal business metrics. These metrics are not in the must-have or should-have category, rather they are fall into the good-to-have category, and may be able to provide some correlation to resource metrics.

Baseline Metric performance character during normal operations.

Business Metrics These are the user or transactional activity based metrics that are responsible for driving the utilization of the infrastructure resources. Also, it is the increase in the business metric measurement that drives the need to increase the infrastructure capacity. Any business system must have at least one business metric. Business metrics can be classified as either principal or auxiliary.

Capacity The maximum value an IT service/component metric can deliver without breaching the service level agreement/target. It is also called capacity limit or maximum capacity.

Capacity Driver The business metrics driving the IT system infrastructure resources utilization.

Capacity Management The information technology risk management process for ensuring there is adequate infrastructure and computing resources to meet the current and future demand of the business in a cost effective and timely manner.

Capacity Management Maturity Model A model that shows the different organizational implementation levels of the capacity management process and the measure of its value and proactiveness.

Capacity plan A document outlining the future business demand, as well as the infrastructure and computing resources needed to meet this demand. It also includes the business scenarios, assumptions, options and costs.

Capacity Planning A component/activity within the capacity management process responsible for the production of capacity plan.

Capacity Risk The possibility of suffering IT service failure or performance degradation as a result of insufficient infrastructure or computing resources.

Concurrent Request The ability of a system to support simultaneous requests from users, usually, metrics related to this falls within the principal metric type.

Content Request The ability of a system to support the delivery of content to users.

Critical Success factor Something that needs to be in place for a process or activity is to succeed.

Data Aggregation The process by which detailed datasets or metrics are expressed in summary for use in making capacity management decisions.

Data Collection The capacity management activity of measuring and gathering data related to metrics usage.

Data Resolution Applies to data collection and aggregation.

Demand Management Optimizing the use of limited infrastructure and computing resource by ensuring that priority is given to critical users and activities.

Derived Metrics Metric that their values are obtained using other base metrics, for example, Memory Utilization (%) = 100 - Available Memory (%). "Memory Utilization (%)" metric is derived from the base metric "Available Memory (%)".

Dominic's Model The diagram of the Capacity Management Process Model based on the author's view.

Firewall A network security system with predetermined rules for monitoring and controlling incoming and outgoing network traffic.

Hard aggregation A term introduced in this book to denote the technique in capacity database where the aggregated data value is computed and stored in the database.

Hard Capacity Limit A term introduced in this book; unlike soft capacity limit, hard capacity limit is fixed, and utilization cannot exceed this limit. However, hitting the limit will definitely lead to performance issue. For example, a server with 128GB RAM Memory, and 1TB hard drive installed- will have hard capacity limit of 128GB and 1TB respectively.

Hardware A collection of the physical components of an information System.

Incident An unplanned interruption to an IT service, either as performance degradation or complete outage.

IOSTATS (input/output statistics) is a Unix operating system inbuilt command, for monitoring the system's storage input and output usage statistics.

IT Service One or more software applications that deliver business requirements.

IT system Request Types IT System requests can be classified into 3 types namely: concurrency, persistence or content.

Mainframe Also called "big iron" is a powerful, multiuser computer that is able to support thousands of users concurrently.

Maximum Capacity The maximum value an IT service/component metric can deliver without breaching the service level agreement/target. It is also called capacity limit or maximum capacity.

Measurement The magnitude or actual reading of a capacity driver, and should be associated with a unit.

Metric A periodic point in time measurement of a specific aspect of a process.

Metric Usage The metric's absolute measurement value.

Metric Usage (%) Metrics usage in percentage is based on the ratio between absolute measurement value and the metrics maximum measurement (capacity limit value).

Modelling Any technique used to predict future utilization of a metric.

Performance The ability of an IT system to meet the timeliness requirement of users. Basically, response time, throughput and concurrency measures are means of determining the performance of an IT system or component.

Persistence Request The ability of a system to store data, and serve generated content for users

Principal Business Metrics A term introduced in this book for describing the business metrics that really drive the IT system's infrastructure resource utilization. Ideally, any IT system must have at least one principal business metric.

Processor Queue Length The number of threads waiting for the processor.

Reporting Time Zone The time zone that an organization adopts as initial global reporting time zone for the purpose of determining global peak.

Resource Metrics System metrics relating to the infrastructures on which an IT service runs e.g. CPU, Memory, disk space, etc.

Response Time How long a request or task takes to get completed.

Scalability The ability of an IT system or component to maintain its performance characteristics as the business workload increases.

Server A computer that shares its resources and information with others computing infrastructures across a network.

Service level Agreement (SLA) This is an agreement between an IT service provider and the customer (the business user). In capacity management, the SLA is based on performance expected from an IT service.

Service Metrics These are metrics that measures the performance of an IT system for a target IT services. The focus is on the service throughput and latency and it is a key component for SLA negotiation.

Service Time The amount of time spent in using an infrastructure or computing resource, when the workload is a single transaction.

Soft Aggregation A term introduced in this book to denote the technique in capacity database where the aggregated data value is dynamically computed when required and not stored in database.

Soft Capacity Limit A term introduced in this book; unlike hard capacity limit, soft capacity limit is a virtual capacity and can be changed within the CDB when deemed appropriate. Also, it can be breached with little or no performance issue. Usually, it is associated with business metrics, until the metrics' actual capacity value are worked out.

Software In contrast to the physical hardware, software is a collection of encoded information or instructions that enables users to interact and perform tasks with the computer

Threshold Metric usage point at which when exceeded should indicate a concern as the continued trend can lead to incident occurring.

Threshold alert A warning that a set threshold has been breached.

Throughput The rate at which requests to an IT system are completed, usually measured as total operations done over a unit time e.g. 100 downloads/sec.

UnlimitedAnalytics A data analytics, business intelligence and capacity management software (www.UnlimitedAnalytics.com).

User A person or another system using an IT system. A user can be internal or external to an organization.

D

P

percentile aggregation method · 33, 91, 92

performance metrics · xix, 21, 44, 63, 70, 84, 85, 217

   cpu · 215

   external · 42

   I/O and transfer · 216

   internal · 42

   memory · 215

   paging · 216

performance restraint resources · 151

performance testing · 39, 79, 81, 134

   load testing · 81

   single thread workload · 83

   soak testing · 82

   stress testing · 82

persistence · 138, 158, 161, 229

problem management · 24, 34

Q

qlikview · 73

R

raw data · 33, 105

release management · 21

reliability · 104

resource data collection · 41, 49, 51

   absolute vs. utilization value · 55

   agent-less or agent-based · 49

   technologies · 49

   unix - iostat utility · 217

   unix - sar utility · 214

   unix - vmstat utility · 211

   Windows – Logman.exe · 219

resource metrics · 229

resource utilization forecast · 162

response types · 187

retention · 105

r-squared · 143

S

scalability · 108, 229

scatter · 117

service level agreement · 16

service level management · 23

service metrics · 38, 230

service performance · 26, 66, 133, 134

   latency · 42, 46

   throughput · 46

   throughput · 6, 32, 42

Splunk · 73

Storage Area Network (SAN) · 45, 56, 150, 189

storage technique · 99

stripping · 105

supply · 4, 5

system resource utilization overview · 47

T

team organization · 28

telephony · 19, 46

threshold alerting · 187

U

W

CPSIA information can be obtained
at www.ICGtesting.com
Printed in the USA
LVOW09s0753141217
559686LV00017B/388/P